Landmarks of Rochester and Monroe County

A York State Book

Landmarks of

Landmark Society of Western New York, *Sponsor*

Rochester and Monroe County:

A Guide to Neighborhoods and Villages

PAUL MALO

Photographs by HANS PADELT and Others

SYRACUSE UNIVERSITY PRESS   1974

Library of Congress Cataloging in Publication Data

Malo, Paul.
    Landmarks of Rochester and Monroe County.

    Bibliography: p.
    1. Monroe Co., N. Y.—Historic houses, etc.
2. Rochester, N. Y.—Historic houses, etc.   3. Archi-
tecture—Monroe Co., N. Y.   4. Architecture—Monroe
Co., N. Y.—Conservation and preservation.   I. Land-
mark Society of Western New York.   II. Title.
NA730.N42M666   1974   917.47'88'03   73-23095
ISBN 0-8153-0103-4
ISBN 0-8153-0104-2 (pbk.)

Manufactured in the United States of America

CONTENTS

Paul Malo is Professor of Architecture at Syracuse University, where he teaches architectural design and has taught architectural history. He is a practicing architect and is co-author of *Architecture Worth Saving in Onondaga County*. He has been a consultant throughout New York State on preservation and adaptive use of areas and buildings.

Hans Padelt, inventor of the Graflex-XL camera and a widely known photographer, is an artist as well as a skilled technician, as the photographs in this book illustrate. Mr. Padelt was a senior engineer at the Graflex Company in Rochester from 1951 to 1969, when he retired to Nova Scotia. He was previously a free-lance camera design consultant and a professional photographer in Dresden, Germany.

PREFACE

Several years of association with the Landmark Society of Western New York have preceded the preparation of this book. As a member and consultant of the Landmark Society, I have collaborated with other members and consultants, as well as staff, in adaptive use studies for individual buildings; extensive area surveys; the preparation of lectures, exhibitions, and educational projects; and the preparation of urban design, land use, and historic district legislation.

This book is not intended primarily to be about its sponsor, the Landmark Society, but it will soon be evident that appreciation for the environment of Monroe County requires frequent reference to this remarkable organization and its work. Furthermore, the Landmark Society is recognized nationally for its regional leadership in historic preservation and environmental conservation.

The Society for the Preservation of Landmarks in Western New York was founded in 1937. Like many older preservation organizations, it originated with the saving of an important building, the Campbell-Whittlesey House in Rochester (Plates 77–79). The early history of the society is largely the story of acquiring and restoring this building, then of making it significant to the community. With educational programs and active participation of volunteers, the base of membership grew, until the organization was confident enough to acquire other properties. Realizing that maintenance as museums could not provide preservation for every historic property, the society developed varied programs of adaptive use, sometimes by leasing buildings to others. Resale with restrictive covenants also has been utilized. The society has become involved in urban design and planning; this will be discussed in chapters on the East Avenue and Third Ward areas of Rochester.

The visual quality of this book is due largely to our singular fortune: the working collaboration of Hans Padelt. As the inventor of the Graflex-XL camera, his understanding of its capabilities is evidenced by the almost one hundred photographs he has taken expressly for this book. The most effective light falls on a building only at a certain hour, depending upon its orientation. Considerable planning and patience are required to portray structures at all corners of a county under ideal conditions of season, weather, and time of day. For over a year Hans Padelt worked on this project, often carrying with him a screwdriver to remove screen doors from fine old Federal entrances, sometimes requesting that protective winter coverings be removed from garden beds in the spring or that the police stop traffic on a busy street. The several photographs by others attain the high standards of Hans Padelt; in one instance, rather than attempting another photograph of a particular subject, Padelt said he would not try to improve upon John Wenrich's picture. Locally made camera, film, and processing materials were used; this visual portrayal of Rochester and Monroe County should be a credit to the local photographic industry and to the artistic as well as the economic role of photography in the community.

For photographs not taken by Hans Padelt, acknowledgment is made as follows:

The Walrus studio for Case Building (Plate 9) and Commerce Building (Plate 10).

Josephson Studio for Rochester Savings Bank (Plate 49).

Linn Duncan for Eastman Theater (Plate 53).

Balthazar Korab for Midtown Plaza interior (Plate 54).

Earl W. Kage for Campbell-Whittlesey House interior, stair (Plate 78).

Photographer not known for Campbell-Whittlesey House interior, west parlor (Plate 79) from *Good Housekeeping*, May, 1960.

John A. Wenrich for Mount Hope Cemetery (Plate 87), David Lee House, Clarkson (Plate 94), Morgan-Manning House, Brockport (Plate 97), and 37 Ontario Street, Honeoye Falls (Plate 6).

Chalmer Alexander for Rochester Institute of Technology (Plate 98).

The old illustrations of the Powers Building (Plates 58 and 59) are included through the courtesy of Dr. Blake McKelvey and the Rochester Public Library.

The maps were drawn by John Fonda, cartographer at Syracuse University.

The New York State Council on the Arts has assisted many of the activities of the Landmark Society, including the preparation of this book. Thanks largely to the support of the New York State Council on the Arts, during the past decade several publications have appeared in the informal county-by-county series known as *Architectecture Worth Saving in New York State*. Monroe County, containing the city of Rochester, is the most populous and urban county yet to be portrayed.

Much of the research for this book was done voluntarily by members and staff of the Landmark Society. Mrs. Patrick Harrington, executive director of the society, has inspired this and other projects of the organization. The Landmark Society is the ultimate author, as well as the patron, of this book.

Paul Malo

School of Architecture
Syracuse University
Autumn 1973

1

INTRODUCTION

Monroe County, in western New York, is bounded on the north by Lake Ontario. It is gently rolling country, rural at its margins, but dominated by the central, expanding city and suburbs of Rochester. There was little settlement here or elsewhere in New York State west of the Hudson-Mohawk river system prior to the nineteenth century. Titles to lands were transferred from Indians to settlers and developers mostly after the Revolutionary War. In the first quarter of the nineteenth century, turnpikes and canals made upstate, interior counties more accessible, generally to migration from the east. Fertile land and a climate tempered by the lake attracted agricultural development. Water power and transportation encouraged diversified light industry and regional commerce.

Rochester grew quickly, becoming the third city in the state. Unlike some communities, its wealth stayed largely at home. Rochester became known as a prosperous and rather contented middle-class, middle-sized city. As its weather has favored horticulture, commercial nurseries, public parks, and private gardens have been prominent. Magnificent trees are among the treasures inherited from the past century and a half. The wealth of the community has encouraged the arts, particularly music, for which the city has become famous. Prosperity also has been expressed in architecture; several local designers merit recognition, and others of international repute have left major works here.

Even lifelong residents of Monroe County may be rewarded by looking again at familiar surroundings, especially if old things are seen as new, in the way that they are discovered by visitors. This book, arranged as a tour, is designed to serve as an introductory guide to the county. There is no need to follow the circuit in sequence. In all, it is an itinerary requiring several days.

Of many approaches to the city, one of the more traversed is from the east. Most visitors today arrive by automobile, and the proposed route begins at the easternmost of the Rochester exits from the New York State Thruway, as shown on the county map. Now that new arterial highways have supplanted older routes, one may hasten from the countryside directly to the downtown, with little awareness of environs. To better appreciate the transition from rural to urban, and from past to present, a good place to stop first is the Village of Pittsford. East Avenue, rich in architecture and cultural institutions, leads to downtown Rochester. Nearby are the Third Ward and Mount Hope districts. For the unhurried observer, this much may be more than a full day's itinerary, particularly if the several museums are visited, as well as the interiors of other buildings open to the public.

As shown on the county map, a drive is suggested by the scenic lake route to the western part of the county, and the villages of Clarkson and Brockport. The new campus of the Rochester Institute of Technology may be seen on the way to Scottsville, and the Genesee Country Museum at Mumford, in the extreme southwest corner of the county. The circuit may be completed by way of Honeoye Falls. This rural tour also may require more than a full day, if the pace is leisurely. Visitors should allow three days to see everything from Pittsford to Honeoye Falls at a comfortable pace. Residents of the county can see these places more frequently and conveniently, and they may not require such an itinerary.

Most of the places to be seen are privately owned, and constant intrusion of unannounced visitors becomes annoying to residents. Where interiors or grounds may be viewed by the public, it is indicated. Otherwise, visitors ought to respect the privacy of occupants, limiting their viewing to the exterior as seen from the street. On occasion many of these places are opened for special events or by prior arrangement by groups or individuals. The Landmark Society serves as a clearing house for these arrangements, and inquiries should be addressed to that organization at 130 Spring Street, Rochester, New York 14608.

This book has been arranged geographically to enable the observer to appreciate better an environment that has largely been inherited from the past. If the arrangement were chronological and the focus were upon isolated objects in the context of their own time, appreciation of the present environment might be missed. Old buildings are valuable not only for their association with earlier times but also for their place in the surroundings in which we live.

We have been interested in the character of residential neighborhoods, the vitality of the downtown, the scenic quality of the countryside, as well as with individual monuments of historic architecture. There is an accumulative value to aggregations of things, so that the total worth may be more than the sum of the parts, considered separately. Many attractive residential streets are comprised of buildings that are unexceptional when considered individually, just as an exciting commercial district may be composed largely of undistinguished works of architecture. Besides considering individual buildings of distinctive worth, we hope to convey agreeable relationships even among those less important buildings.

There is a harmony, an identity, a sense of place in certain areas and districts. It may be of greater worth to future generations to preserve the character of neighborhoods from environmental homogenization than to save a few notable buildings. To our heirs, a modest old street like Portsmouth Terrace may be as valuable as the Eastman House, a national monument.

The needs, desires, capabilities and limitations, values, and lifestyles of our predecessors can be known from our mixed surroundings. If the world in which we live is somewhat an accident of history, the variety and surprise of the accidental contribute to its delight.

Because the City of Rochester and its metropolitan environs dominate the county, the emphasis in this book may be more urban than rural. Yet, Monroe County contains many unspoiled country landscapes and attractive villages. Of these, we have selected only a few as representative. The growth of a metropolis creates special problems of preservation and conservation. These have been a concern of the Landmark Society and many town, village, and neighborhood groups in the county. Although there are some discussions of case histories, strategies, and techniques of area preservation, this book is not a "how-to" manual. Rather, it is intended to evoke the qualities of Monroe County surroundings and to widen the appreciation of them.

It has not been possible to record all of the historic architecture in Monroe County or to represent every building type. If an imbalance favors houses, it is because of their intimate association with the lives of their builders, as well as their present occupants, and their preponderance in our surroundings. Some building types, such as churches, may have less representation than they deserve. Nevertheless, they may be better known and appreciated in the community than many other building types and, with the exception of some inner-city religious buildings, may be better assured of preservation.

More utilitarian buildings such as barns, warehouses, and even some good industrial buildings might have been included since these comprise a part of a region's history and may be well-designed, handsome structures in themselves. Nevertheless, with the basic organization as a tour, examples have been selected from groupings in neighborhoods that could be visited within a restricted circuit. Many fine individual but out-of-the-way structures have not been mentioned, just as many valuable and attractive areas in the county could not be represented.

The definitive record of a century and a half of building in Monroe County is yet to be compiled. There has been some specialized interest locally in cobblestone construction, with a society devoted to its study. Genuine contributions to regional architectural history have been made by scholars such as Carl Schmidt; the art historian Professor Carl Hersey of the University of Rochester has expanded appreciation of the architectural heritage here; Dr. Blake McKelvey is without peer as the general historian of the county and is widely known as an urban historian. Many town historians also have contributed to research on this book. Nevertheless, despite the considerable work already done by these authorities and by the staff and volunteers of the Landmark Society, the full recording and evaluation, the complete environmental history of Monroe County, remains to be written, as it continues to be made.

2

ARCHITECTURE IN MONROE COUNTY:

A Historical Survey

Because this book has been arranged geographically rather than chronologically, a discussion of architectural styles in historical sequence may be useful.

The Federal style prevailed from the earliest settlement here in the last decades of the eighteenth century until well after the opening of the Erie Canal, through the 1830s (Plate 1). Most surviving buildings of the earliest period are houses, built of either brick or wood, although the Phoenix Hotel (Plate 14) in Pittsford is an important early commercial building. The Federal style reflected late and post-Georgian, English tastes. Sometimes called "post-Colonial" in this country, it was derived from the elegant work of the Adams' and their contemporaries in England, and corresponded to the Regency style of the early nineteenth century in that country. Refinement of classical elements into thin and attenuated forms was characteristic of this taste. Upstate New York work followed that of New England, as most early settlers came from there. Even frontier pioneers aspired to elegance: delicate cornices, moldings, entrance doorways, fireplaces, and stairways graced early buildings.

1. *Federal style:* **Simeon B. Jewett House,** 3779 Lake Road, Clarkson, 1828.

7

2. *Greek Revival style:* **Elihu Kirby House,** 22 Stoney Clover Lane, Pittsford, 1840. It was moved and restored in 1956 by Mr. and Mrs. Richard Turner. Walter Cassebeer, supervising architect. Fletcher Steele, landscape architect.

Well into the second quarter of the nineteenth century, a new building style swept the region. The more monumental and imposing classical forms of the Greek Revival replaced Federal models, which perhaps had finally become over-refined, or at least over-familiar. Although in practice sometimes grandiose, the Greek Revival, in contrast to the reticence of the Federal style, strived for epic grandeur (Plate 2). Endorsed by such a national hero as President Jefferson, the classical revival was partially a reaction of the new Republic against cultural dominance by older, aristocratic English tastes and traditions. Just as the adoption of trousers, replacing satin breeches, symbolized democratic sympathies at the time, so the Athenian image became American. As it was then said of the people that "General Jackson is *their own* President," so classical Greek architecture was enthusiastically rediscovered and made native. Remote farmhouses became white temples, even if built of wood.

The new vision looked more for large effects than small refinements. Monumental scale could be attained by nailing together machine-sawed boards; for fine, hand-crafted detail, the new style often substituted cheaper and sometimes gross work. But often the vision was noble, expressing newly realized power and confidence.

Even before the Civil War, American culture was changing. Victoria had come to the throne decades earlier in England, marking the advent of a stylistic era bearing her name. Nevertheless, the classical rule declined gradually here. In later Greek Revival examples, there appear increasingly richer, more inventive, and less historically correct features, such as elaborate eaves brackets on the exterior and heavy plaster ceiling moldings on the interior. Although buildings still classical in form commonly were built into the second half of the century, the flowering of the Greek Revival style locally may be considered to occupy the 1840s.

In Monroe County, the earlier Federal tradition was not supplanted altogether by the Greek Revival, but continued concurrently as a strong influence, especially in outlying areas. The familiar doorways with elliptical fanlights and the small eaves cornices of the earlier style appear in new work through the mid-century, at the same time Greek Revival buildings were appearing. Only a final transformation of taste occurring with the Civil War seems to have subverted this long-lived, generic tradition. About three decades after that war, moreover, the first wave of Colonial Revivalism rediscovered this traditional style, which continues in popularity locally.

Contrary to this rather conservative, traditional mainstream, there was, in the mid-nineteenth century, a current flowing afar in search of the exotic. Romanticism yearned for new levels of emotional consciousness, and the medieval Gothic style, long disfavored, now was considered to be "sublime." Its use was actively encouraged by liturgical conservatives in the Episcopal church. St. Luke's Church (Plates 67 and 69) in Rochester is an early example of 1824. Fewer houses and other building types were rendered in this style, because it never attained the widespread popularity of the Greek Revival. However, several good Gothic Revival houses remain. For many churches, the Gothic has continued to seem appropriate until recent times. The Ellwanger and Barry Nursery Office (Plates 3 and 83), by the nationally prominent architect A. J. Davis, is one of the most important regional examples of the style. Although St. Luke's Church preceded most work here even of Greek Revival character, the Gothic Revival is more commonly associated with the later mid-century, when the Greek influence was on the wane.

The Greek and Gothic were precursors of other nineteenth-century revivals and foreign influences. About mid-century, the model of the Italian

3. *Gothic Revival style:* **Ellwanger and Barry Nursery Office,** 668 Mount Hope Avenue, Rochester, 1854. Alexander Jackson Davis, architect.

country villa became popular, supposedly imported from Tuscany (Plate 4). The term "Italianate" was used at the time for a style with vertical proportions, tall windows, and low hipped roofs with broadly overhanging, usually bracketed eaves. Often a house was surmounted with a windowed cupola, or embellished with a square tower. The roofs of extensive verandas generally were carried by elaborate square columns, set on pedestals, sometimes joined by balustrades.

Cosmopolitan American taste at the time of the Civil War looked also to Second Empire France (Plate 5). The mansard roof became a familiar feature of the French mode. Although there was considerable similarity to the Italianate, especially in emphasized verticality, richness of ornament (usually rather heavy) was more characteristic of the Second Empire—the quality often associated in this country with the term "Victorian."

Many hybrids flowered from this mixed stylistic stock. Only recently have we begun to recognize characteristic strains with identifiable antecedents, as seen in many of the buildings around us. As a whole, the post–Civil War period is popularly characterized by an opulence that sometimes surpassed propriety and became ostentation. This change in taste reflected a basic change in the economy, the society, and the culture of the time. Only a few decades earlier the county had been rural; it had looked to well-established models and values, largely agrarian, of the eighteenth century. Suddenly this was transformed. Developing resources of power, population, and transportation, new commerce and industry created new wealth. Cities such as Rochester boomed, and with them appeared a new urban culture. Between the white Greek village house (Plate 99) and the brown mansard city mansion (Plate 80), there is an enormous difference in kind, yet there may be only a decade or so difference between their construction dates.

Innovation and novelty were prized in the later nineteenth century. Fidelity to historical models of Gothic, Italian, or French origin (until the turn of the century) was less significant than inventive adaptation. In this

4. *Italianate style:* **George D. Southworth House,** 1883 Penfield Road, Penfield, 1878.

14

way the era of Victoria recalled that of Elizabeth. By the final quarter of the century, a new language of design had evolved. The name of the reforming English furniture designer Eastlake is sometimes associated with the leaner, more angular manifestations; there is a recognizable American species (the term "stick style" has been used). This was mainly a residential characteristic of the 1870s. Frame houses of picturesque composition and elaborate form, steep roofs, and rather flat walls (sometimes with decorative banding) were contrasted with complex (usually machine-made) decoration of gables, porches, and, sometimes, window lintels, often of a skeletal, spiny form. An example of the Eastlake style is shown in Plate 6.

During the 1880s an indirect influence of historical Romanesque examples, especially as freely interpreted by the great contemporary American architect H. H. Richardson, produced a somewhat simpler and less agitated style, which has been termed "Richardsonian." This work evidenced similar fondness for richly sculptural masses and complex interior spaces, combined with rather bold use of natural materials. However, in contrast to the lean English Eastlake style, Richardson's style, like himself, was robust and rotund. Round arches derived from the Romanesque were combined with rounded wall forms—usually of rough stone in his public buildings. This influence is seen in the Third Presbyterian Church and the Soule House (Plates 34 and 35), both on East Avenue, and in the old Federal Building downtown (Plates 64 and 65). In his residential work Richardson often substituted wood shingles for stone, retaining the same sort of full-bodied forms.

5. *Second Empire style:* **Henry A. DeLand House,** 99 South Main Street, corner of Church Street, Fairport, c. 1876.

The name "shingle style" has been applied to these fairly plain but sculptural houses, often combining field stone and other natural materials. Grace Episcopal Church (Plate 7), Scottsville, represents this type of design. The climate of this period nurtured the later talents of Louis Sullivan and Frank Lloyd Wright, towards the turn of the century.

Richard Norman Shaw, another brilliant English designer, influenced avant-garde American taste in the 1880s. The eccentric residence at 727 East Avenue (Plate 38) is very much a Shaw inspiration, combining a disparate collection of elements drawn from many sources into a novel, artistic composition. Probably the work of Shaw himself was known at the time only to a few cultivated American designers such as Rochester's Harvey Ellis. Shaw's influence, however, surrounds us with many buildings of the "Queen Anne style." Unlike the more restrained work of the Queen Anne period, American work following Shaw's example is typified by a rather stout house of chunky form, usually with bulging bay windows and other projections of upper floors and massive roofs contributing to a top-heavy look.

Like simple frame barns, many nineteenth-century urban structures designed to be utilitarian attained beauty through the simple and forceful use of materials. Mills, breweries, and similar functional buildings often were handsome in appearance, like the warehouse at 1 Mount Hope Avenue (Plate 8), with an interior of heavy timber construction combined with exterior stone bearing walls. Towards the end of the century, new means of construction and the invention of elevators made possible new types of commercial buildings, with their own characteristic forms. The skyscraper caught the popular imagination. New materials—cast iron and, later, steel—suggested

6. *Eastlake style:* **37 Ontario Street,** Honeoye Falls, c. 1875.

new architectural forms. Downtown Rochester retains several fine buildings that represent evolving construction techniques. The Powers Building (Plates 58–62, and 63) was begun right after the Civil War, in 1869. The Case Building of 1882–83 (Plate 9), by Louis P. Rogers, is another good example of cast iron construction exposed on the exterior. In 1888 the Wilder Building (Plate 63) became the tallest in town. In employing new techniques of construction, Rochester was in the forefront, among the most technically advanced cities in the country.

The Chicago World's Fair of 1893 marked a transformation in taste almost as complete as had the Civil War. For decades, newly emerging and influential architects of the eastern cities, many professionally educated in Paris, had been employing more academically correct, historical styles, largely classical. It was the dominance of their taste in the design of the World's Columbian Exposition, the "Great White City" of Chicago, that popularly revived more traditional forms, particularly those of classical, Renaissance, and baroque European models. The fair was immensely popular and served as effective propaganda for European eclectic classicism. In Monroe County it resulted in such splendid works as the third Monroe County Courthouse (Plates 66 and 68), which is now the County Office Building, and the Eastman Theater (Plate 53). Its influence on the high-rise office building may be seen in the richly elaborated Commerce Building (Plate 10), built in 1894 and designed by Nolan, Nolan and Stern.

At the time it probably appeared that the national admiration for the spectacular Chicago World's Fair would result in a consolidation of taste into a neoclassical renaissance. This almost happened. As the twentieth century began, the mainstream of architectural design followed the lead of the more academically (and usually European) educated architects of the East Coast, adapting historical styles to modern needs. Much of this work, of excellent quality and genuine taste, is evident in Monroe County. The Watson Library (Plate 44) on Prince Street, by the New York architect John du Fais, is an

7. *Richardsonian style:* **Grace Episcopal Church,** Browns Avenue, Scottsville, 1885. Charles and Harvey Ellis, architects.

8. *Stone and timber commercial construction:* **Stone Warehouse,** 1 Mount Hope Avenue, Rochester, c. 1822. The original owners were Myron Holley and John Gilbert.

excellent example, deriving from eighteenth-century French practice. With the Chicago World's Fair also came a neo-Colonial renaissance, which has continued locally well into this century. The general term "eclecticism" is used to refer to this historically derivative school of design, which found models from many periods of architectural history for new buildings of the early twentieth century.

Native inventiveness and independence, however, were not to be suppressed. A secondary and more turbulent current, opposed to the mainstream, continued from the earlier nineteenth century. More than a decorative fashion, it was a matter of ideology. A philosophical attitude toward design, often reinforced by strong moral convictions, derived from the nineteenth-century theories and sermons of Ruskin and Morris in England about "honest" design. The arts and crafts movement in England reached the United States and combined with a native critical attitude of common sense. From the decades of Eastlake and Richardson in the 1870s and 1880s, a new tradition, a new attitude towards design, had been forming. In Chicago, where a distinctive, nonhistorical commercial architecture was well developed, Louis Sullivan foresaw the World's Fair as a retrogressive influence on native American design. His junior, Frank Lloyd Wright persisted on his independent course. When his Boynton House (Plates 31 and 32) was built in Rochester in 1907, his work already was unique and radically opposed to the prevalent taste.

During the first decade of the twentieth century, the Rochester architect Claude Bragdon was developing his personal style. Although more of a transitionalist than a revolutionist such as Wright, he was continuing the sort of innovations introduced by Richard Norman Shaw and Harvey Ellis, freely combining traditional forms. The First Universalist Church (Plates 56 and 57) is Bragdon's finest remaining work, since the tragic demolition of the New York Central Station. Some commercial buildings of this decade, such as the local architect J. Foster Warner's Sibley store of 1904 (Plates 47 and 48), were continuing modern experiments.

9. *Cast iron commercial architecture:* **Case Building,** 82 St. Paul Street, Rochester, 1882–83. Louis P. Rogers, architect. The orginal owner was H. H. Warner, Rochester's patent medicine king.

In Europe, evangelistic sermons from England about "honesty" in design reached the continent. Europe also noticed pioneering American design, particularly of tall commercial buildings, as well as the emerging personal style of Wright. The American export returned a decade or so later as a more doctrinaire style, an imported "modern" architecture. Labeled some time ago (seemingly with more optimism than reason) the "international style," it was of little significance in this country until the end of the Second World War. Some distinguished European architects had migrated to this country during the war period and contributed to the post-war era of building.

Modern architecture was neither imported nor rediscovered. In fact, the sort of independent work being done during the first decade of this century continued. Perhaps it was mostly restricted to projects that supposedly were more "practical," such as the additions to the Sibley store (Plates 47 and 48). Public schools were among the earlier building types to employ a less affected, functional style. Pittsford retains an excellent example, the Lincoln Avenue School of 1916.

During the 1920s and 1930s, falling somewhere between the historical revivalism practiced by one school of architects, who were influenced by older European traditions, and the radical machinelike "functionalism" that was supposed to be developing in modern Europe, was the work of many American designers. Perhaps it is best suggested by a term of the time, "modernistic." The familiar winged forms of the Times Square Building on the Rochester skyline (Plate 11), like the Public Library, recall a taste of the 1920s and 1930s for forms that were neither historical in detail nor startlingly unfamiliar. A taste for ornamental enrichment continued, and a system of ornament developed, now called "Art Deco." If there is a single element to recall its prevalence, the zig-zag, chevron, or lightning-bolt device best seems to represent the era. A building like the Public Library also might be seen as "streamlined classical." The Times Square Building seems to be more formally creative, particularly its sculptural tower, although basically it also is composed in a traditional, symmetrical manner. Built in 1929 as the Genesee Valley Trust Building, it was designed by Voorhees, Gmelin and Walker of New York, with Carl C. Ade.

Because of the Depression, followed by the Second World War, two decades of the twentieth century were not marked by local building so much as were earlier and later periods. But after the war, what now is recognized as "modern" architecture began to appear more regularly. Commercial buildings naturally continued in the modern idiom, which began to find some acceptance as well for churches and other public buildings. The Asbury Methodist Church on East Avenue (Plate 34) is a transitional example, while the local architect James H. Johnson more recently has designed some distinctive modern religious buildings (Plate 22). Even a few houses have been built that break from the usual preference for historical association, such as the Robert H. Antell House (Plate 12), completed in 1971 and designed by James H. Johnson.

More generally, domestic taste in recent decades has been rather conservative, or at least the speculative builders seem to have gauged it to be so. Of course, home owners generally must select from what house builders make available to them. Banks frequently have built new branches in mock-Colonial style, apparently also judging this to be best suited to their customers. Some outlying post offices and churches—even shopping centers and gas stations—have been embellished with shutters and cupolas. While appreciation for historical buildings and a conscious effort to harmonize with them are laudable, the fabrication of fake historical buildings often is ill-advised.

Because subsequent generations have left works of differing character, the environment of Monroe County has been enriched. If the development of new forms in our own time is repressed by admiration for the past, the future may be deprived of a fitting contribution. Most probably our grandchildren and their children will consider James Johnson's churches and houses to be

10. *Eclectic classicism:* **Commerce Building,** 119 East Main Street, Rochester, 1894. Nolan, Nolan and Stern, architects. The original owner was William S. Kimball, tobacco manufacturer.

11. *Rochester Towers:* **St. Luke's Episcopal Church** (1824), **City Hall** (1874–75), and the **Times Square Building** (1929) as seen from Broad Street (the old Erie Canal), Rochester.

12. *Modern residential innovation:* **Robert H. Antell House,** 142 Park Road, Pittsford, 1971. James H. Johnson, architect.

more valuable expressions of the mid-twentieth century than they will some of the tasteful neo-Georgian buildings that continue to be built.

Despite a general suburban conservatism, it now seems, after the first half of the twentieth century, that there is indeed an architecture of our own time. The 1960s was the greatest decade of urban development in Rochester since the 1920s, and construction continues. The best recent buildings seem to be characteristically American, integrating many tendencies evident in the national past. The new towers on the Rochester skyline (Plates 13, 55, and 56), although basically the same in function and construction, by their contrast suggest a continuing restlessness after another solution to even the most familiar problem—a desire to be independent, individual, and innovative. The new campus of the Rochester Institute of Technology (Plate 98), certainly one of the regional masterworks of our time, returns to the familiar local brick of Pittsford and Clarkson, reinterpreting masonry forms in a way that is neither immitative of the past nor startlingly strange. While some of the experiments of the young architect James Johnson may seem bizarre, such a designer represents a healthy aspect of the present county scene. Despite an innovative history, Monroe County today, as in the past, seems to be characterized less by a desire to impress, to astonish, or to evidence fashion consciousness than it has been, and it continues to be characterized by a more contented appreciation for quality.

Viewing the way the county environment has been enriched by some

13. *Modern commercial architecture:* **Lincoln First Bank Building,** 1 Lincoln First Square, Rochester, 1973. John Graham and Company, New York, architects.

eight generations, one is impressed not only that Frank Lloyd Wright came here to build a house in 1907, or that other distinguished architects from afar have been called to build the best buildings possible; one is also impressed that Rochester has produced such native architects as the Warners (father and son), Harvey Ellis, Claude Bragdon, James Johnson, and many others, and has given them appreciative clients. But perhaps most of all, one is impressed by the prevailing quality of design in all periods—most of it anonymous—evidencing that much as it has changed in character from period to period, there has been a high level of taste common to the many generations that have lived in Monroe County.

3

THE VILLAGE OF PITTSFORD

Driving from the New York State Thruway on the eastern expressway, one passes through pleasant, rolling country and soon arrives at Pittsford, one of the oldest communities in Monroe County. The first settlers came to Pittsford in the late eighteenth century, and by 1810 there was a cluster of houses here. The Erie Canal was a major cause of growth, and the waterway still functions as the New York State Barge Canal, which one crosses when approaching the village from the east or north.

At least a brief walking tour of the village is suggested, as outlined here. A more thorough guide to village architecture has been published by Historic Pittsford, Inc., and may be found at the "Little House," a museum of the organization that is open at specified times and is located a few doors down Monroe Avenue from the principal intersection of the village. At other times the booklet may be obtained at the Circulation Office of the Genesee Valley Newspapers, located in the Phoenix Hotel Building, at the principal intersection.

Only steps from the canal, marking the town center, a striking profile of double chimneys and stepped gables identifies the Phoenix Hotel (Plate 14). A tavern was on the site in 1807; the hotel, a larger structure, probably anticipated canal trade, as it is thought to have been built between 1812 and 1824. It served its original purpose as an inn until recent years, when it was handsomely restored to house the offices of a publishing company. The interiors had been altered during a century and a half of use, but some original features remain. Particularly interesting is a large ballroom on the third floor, with an elliptical coved ceiling.

14. Phoenix Hotel, 4 South Main Street, Pittsford. An old inn that served the Erie Canal, this centerpiece for a historic village is Federal in style. The stepped gables framing a fanlight are characteristic, as are the elliptical arches of the lower floor.

Continuing from the principal intersection, walking down Monroe Avenue, one finds many attractive houses, including four important early examples. Beyond the firehouse on the right-hand side of the street is the "Little House." Built in 1819 as a lawyer's office, its diminutive scale characterizes the Federal period.

Next door is an intriguing house (Plate 15). Its surroundings evidence the hand of its owner, the late Fletcher Steele, a landscape architect. Arriving from Connecticut, his family had resided here for generations. The large property extends down to the canal in the rear. The historic house, with its furnishings, was recently willed to the Landmark Society. After considering various alternatives, the society decided that the property should continue to be used as a private residence. It has been sold with a protective covenant assuring its preservation, and the proceeds from this disposition continue the work of the society in other areas.

The arrangement of the house is unusual. The wing projecting to the front, which was added about mid-nineteenth century, continues the style of the older work on the exterior. There are matching porches on each side of the wing, and identical entrance doors opening onto them; each of these entrances has a transom and side lights similar to those seen on the third entrance, into the older portion. Inside the new wing, there is a high, Greek Revival drawing room, linked to the older house by a generous hallway between the two porches.

The wooden balustrades on the roofs are unusual features. Interior variations of floor level result in spatial surprises. As is the case with many of the oldest houses, the kitchen originally was located in the cellar, where a large cooking fireplace remains.

Next door is the 1826 Sylvanus Lathrop House (Plate 16), perhaps the finest of several similar brick houses built in the village during the prosperous decade following construction of the Erie Canal. Lathrop had been one of the builders of the "Great Embankment" of the canal east of Pittsford.

Pre-Greek Revival, the features show the small scale of the late Federal style, influenced by English Regency models. The block device seen on exterior lintels is repeated on the interior woodwork of handsome, formal rooms.

Across the street, at 31 Monroe Avenue, is the similar 1830 Ira Buck House. It is another brick house of a type characteristic of Pittsford. The entrance porch is unusual for its large columns with acanthus-leaved capitals. These may not be original features, as suggested by the larger scale and less traditional form; possibly the porch was reconstructed later in the nineteenth century.

The larger wood frame house next door, at Number 41, was built in 1853 by Dr. Hartwell Carver, a significant figure in the development of transcontinental railroads. It has been enlarged and somewhat altered in more recent times, but it retains much of its mid-nineteenth-century character. The board-and-batten siding and elaborate verge boards, together with steeply pitched roofs and pronounced gables, characterize the Gothic Revival style. Not many houses of this type survive.

The map suggests a route around several blocks; here are many pleasant, smaller houses, typical of the village, as well as the fine frame St. Paul's Lutheran Church on Lincoln Avenue, built in 1884.

On returning to South Main Street, one sees Christ Episcopal Church. This Gothic Revival structure was built in 1868 of Medina sandstone. The attractive red stone underlies most of Western New York State. It was often transported via the Erie Canal from nearby quarries. Because the stone is hard to cut and is therefore expensive, its use has declined. The side and rear portions of the church, although recent additions, are fairly consistent in character with the original work.

Also on South Main Street, a few doors farther from the town center, is the modern St. Louis Roman Catholic Church. To the left of it stands the important Elliot House, a landmark now owned by the church. Built about 1812 by Augustus Elliot, it is another brick building of the Federal style,

15. Fletcher Steele House, 20 Monroe Avenue, Pittsford. Small-scaled Federal detail and irregular form contribute to the special charm of this house. The older portion, to the rear, was built about 1810. Although the projecting wing at the left appears similar in style to the older house, it was built later and was connected to the house by a new entry foyer with matching doorways at either end. Surprisingly, the interior of this wing is one lofty parlor in the Greek Revival style.

with the same kind of stepped gables seen on the Phoenix Hotel (Plate 14). The interiors retain fine features of the Federal style, such as elegant fireplaces with gesso reliefs. The builder's wealth derived from distilling and speculation. The Hargous family of New York subsequently acquired this property as a country seat, entertaining grandly here during the Civil War era. This is one of the most important Federal houses in Monroe County and was altered little, except for additions and the replacement of original, small-paned windows with two-over-two sash later in the nineteenth century. Appreciating the importance of this historic mansion, the church is restoring it.

Returning on South Main Street towards the main intersection, one may note on the left, at Number 25, another house similar to two brick houses of late Federal style that were seen previously. Now used commercially, this brick building was built about 1835 and is the latest of four similar local designs.

A detour around a block before returning to the town center is shown on the map. On Church Street is the cobblestone District No. 6 Schoolhouse of 1842, in more recent times a Masonic Temple (Plate 17). Next door is the 1816 Guetersloh House, still another and probably the earliest of the four similar houses of Federal style characteristic of Pittsford, which have been mentioned. It is the property of the Presbyterian church. The brick, Italianate church building next door was built in 1861 and has received additions through the years. The latest, in 1968, was designed to respect the historic Guetersloh House as well as the century-old church building.

Continuing around the block, one passes several attractive houses, some quite early in date. A Greek Revival frame house is seen at Number 38 State Street, the site of the first log house in the village, built in 1789 by Israel Stone near a natural spring. The building in its present form was made for an Englishman named Plumb in the early nineteenth century, but inside it appears to incorporate portions of older work. Prior to construction of the Erie Canal, there were extensive formal boxwood gardens in the rear.

16. Sylvanus Lathrop House, 28 Monroe Avenue, Pittsford. The late Federal, regional style of the Erie Canal era is well typified by this house, one of several Pittsford houses that are similar in design. Characteristic features of the period include a fine entrance porch, window lintels showing Regency block detail, elliptical gable window, and thin, but broad eaves.

Returning up State Street to the main intersection, one may observe both restoration and reconstruction, and try to guess which of the structures is authentic. One is a historical fiction, designed by the author in the Federal style as a neighbor to a restored frame building. There is some question of whether this solution to a difficult design problem should be encouraged. Nevertheless, by reflecting the simplest and most common style of the Federal period, it aspires to anonymity. It is not an exact reconstruction of a model, although the entrance derives from one found on an old house in a neighboring village, which was measured before its destruction. The fake building is Number 19. Its neighbor at Number 21 has been restored; the entrance here is original. The small cottage to the left, at Number 25, is equally old and awaits restoration.

After returning to the main intersection, one may drive directly to Rochester, taking North Main Street, which again crosses the canal. Immediately beyond the bridge on the right, however, is Schoen Place. This lane along the canal affords a pleasant pause, particularly during the summer months when tugs and barges are passing. This little waterside neighborhood is developing as an appealing area of boutiques, galleries, and specialty shops. The Landmark Society operates the Early Attic Treasures Shop on the corner.

Continuing on North Main Street a short distance, one comes to The Depot (Plate 18), an excellent example of adaptive use. Two good railroad buildings of the nineteenth century, one of brick, the other of wood, have been joined by a modern glass and metal connection. The handsome structure houses a fine restaurant.

On the opposite side of the street is the Hawley-Zornow Homestead, dating from the post–Civil War period. Italianate in style, its cast iron fences are notable, as is the rural setting of open space, retaining a nineteenth-century context for the architecture.

North Main Street becomes East Avenue on leaving the Village of

17. District No. 6 Schoolhouse, 17 Church Street, Pittsford. Cobblestone, often drawn by oxen from the nearby lake shores, is indigenous to Monroe County. The carefully coursed walls, with cut stone used for quoins at the corners and for lintels over openings, are a good example of use of this native material, which was common in the first half of the nineteenth century. Despite the relatively late date (1842), the design shows no Greek Revival influence. Built as a schoolhouse, this substantial structure later became a Masonic Temple.

39

Pittsford; this grand boulevard extends to the heart of Rochester. Before leaving Pittsford, however, a few words should be said about the community and the reasons for its ambiance. It has always been a prosperous village, fairly stable in economy as well as in population. Nevertheless, without the conscious and active concern of its inhabitants throughout the years for maintaining its character, it might have changed into something quite different, particularly at a time when the village has been surrounded by speculative residential and suburban commercial development.

Historic Pittsford, Inc., has been organized to preserve and improve historic and visual quality, and this organization serves its community well. Andrew D. Wolfe has been particularly influential. As the publisher of several local and regional newspapers, his press and his personal example have accomplished much. The restoration of the prime landmark of the community, the Phoenix Hotel, is due to him, as are the removal of an unsightly service station at the principal intersection, the restoration and reconstruction of buildings on State Street, and many other accomplishments, particularly the organization of Historic Pittsford, Inc. As it often happens in community preservation and improvement activities, when a few highly motivated and persistent people are leaders, wide support from the rest of the community follows their initial efforts. Pittsford has become well known as a community that cares about its character and works to maintain and improve it.

18. **The Depot,** 41 North Main Street, Pittsford. An outstanding model of adaptive use is this restaurant of character, which sensitively utilizes the late-nineteenth-century railroad station. Original architectural features, as well as railroad artifacts, have been retained. A minimal glass and metal link connects two old buildings. Like the signs, it evidences restrained taste.

4

PITTSFORD TO DOWNTOWN ROCHESTER:

East Avenue and Its Environs

Rochester, the central city of Monroe County, may be entered by one of the finest gateways to announce any city: East Avenue, which extends from the Village of Pittsford to the Liberty Pole in downtown Rochester. For eight miles it passes through park-like landscape, linking the country with the heart of the city. The grand boulevard passes fine houses, country clubs, churches, colleges, and museums, set on broad lawns, among century-old trees. If many metropolitan areas had them, most such splendid nineteenth-century corridors have been lost to modern commercial development. As a whole, East Avenue comprises perhaps the major historic and visual asset of the region.

An approach to the City of Rochester by the East Avenue corridor always is enhanced by a sense of occasion. There is a processional, almost ceremonial, quality to this entry, dignified by a panoply of historic and architectural monuments, surrounded by verdant gardens and majestic trees. A drive from Pittsford to downtown Rochester should not be hurried—indeed, there are shorter arterial routes for this purpose. These have left East Avenue less crowded and noisy than many major urban avenues. Furthermore, there are many hidden things on side streets off the avenue well worth seeing. In fact, much of the richness of the area is to be found in enclaves that have grown around, but may be screened from, the principal thoroughfare.

Leaving the Village of Pittsford by North Main Street, which becomes East Avenue, one passes through pleasant residential neighborhoods, by two colleges (St. John Fisher and Nazareth) as well as two country clubs. The buildings and, especially, the spacious grounds of these institutions contribute valuably to the attractiveness of the area.

The first detour to be considered by the more leisurely visitor, particularly near mealtime, is to the Spring House (Plate 19), an inn that was built next to the Erie Canal in the early nineteenth century. Although now unfortunately situated in a commercial environment, the historic structure is remarkable. Built of brick like the nearby Phoenix Hotel in Pittsford (Plate 14), which probably preceded it by a few years, the character of the Spring House is quite different. There are typical Federal features, and there also seems to be a basic similarity of form between the Spring House and the several houses of the characteristic Pittsford style previously seen. However, the elaborate development of the portico is much bolder in conception and scale than the usual Federal work. A date on the upper gallery indicates 1822; the Erie Canal was then being constructed, to introduce a new era to the region, and newer architectural forms soon would follow. Already there is a sense of the monumental quality of the Greek Revival. Some alterations and additions have been made. The iron railing and stairs of the exterior, for example, probably are fairly modern. Nevertheless, the building retains its essential form and conveys well the character of an early inn of this type.

Another feature of interest, also located a short distance from East Avenue, is the new Margaret Woodbury Strong Museum. At 700 Allens Creek Road is the estate of the late Mrs. Margaret Woodbury Strong, whose collections are housed in a mansion on spacious grounds there. In her lifetime Mrs. Strong amassed a famous collection of dolls and other artifacts. This museum is not yet open to the public.

Still another place worth searching out is Knollwood Drive, off East Avenue (Plate 20). This inconspicuous lane loops through one of the most attractive residential groupings in the county. The richness of architecture and landscape here suggests a setting for a Scott Fitzgerald novel. The fine house at Number 42 is notable for its design and craftsmanship (Plate 21).

44

Still another short excursion off East Avenue may be made at Penfield Road to visit the unusual Temple Sinai (Plate 22). Built in 1967, it is one of the inventive, modern works of the Rochester architect James H. Johnson. The concrete panels that form both the structural support and the wall enclosure were cast on earth forms and later raised into position. Johnson's work has been characterized by exploration of innovative forms and methods, combined with visual imagination.

The variety and expansiveness of East Avenue is enhanced by the survival of an old farmhouse, one of the oldest in the county (Plates 23 and 24). It was built by Orringh Stone, who acquired the property in 1792. Surrounded by fields and gardens, the Stone-Tolan House, at Number 2370, is a property of the Landmark Society. The Stone-Tolan House is now open to the public on Wednesdays, from 10:00 a.m. to 5:00 p.m., and at other times by appointment or prearranged tours.

Beyond the nearby complex of arterial highways, at the city limits of Rochester, is a small commercial area that grew up around the intersection of East Avenue and Winton Road in the early twentieth century. A short distance from the shopping district, on South Winton Road are two major modern works. Temple Beth El, modeled of brick with baroque vigor by the nationally prominent architect Percival Goodman, was built between 1952 and 1963. Across the street is the First Unitarian Church (Plate 25), another striking brick form, equally sculptural but different in manner. One of Louis I. Kahn's

19. **The Spring House,** 3001 Monroe Avenue, Pittsford. Still functioning as a restaurant, this Erie Canal inn may be compared to the Phoenix Hotel in Pittsford, which represents the early Federal style (Plate 14). The Spring House, built shortly after the Phoenix Hotel, aspired more to monumentality. The portico, with its large columns carrying a massive entablature, forecasted the Greek Revival period. Interior features also have been preserved.

20. Knollwood Drive, Pittsford. The East Avenue gateway to Rochester is park-like for many miles, giving access to hidden enclaves like Knollwood, where fine houses of the early twentieth century are enhanced by magnificent old trees.

major works, the main portion was built in 1962, and the wing to the rear was extended in 1970.

Winton Road defines the city limits of Rochester. Between here and downtown Rochester is the earlier and architecturally the richest residential section of East Avenue. Although a few fine houses have been lost to apartment development, encroaching from Winton Road, most structures of historic value remain. The preservation of this stretch of East Avenue, within the city proper, together with surrounding neighborhoods has not been without problems. An appreciation of the next area to be seen may be enhanced by a brief introduction.

East Avenue has never been bypassed by fashionable favor, but it has been threatened by success. Prestige and attractiveness have created high land values. Restrictive zoning had forestalled much of the high-density, luxury housing and office structures that otherwise would have appeared, but pressures were growing to allow variances or to revise zoning. A few large apartments had already been built, and others were being planned—by persons who anticipated the approval of zoning variance or the adoption of more liberal legislation.

The East Avenue Association and other, smaller neighborhood associations representing the side streets were concerned, as was the Landmark Society. Increasingly, fewer of the large homes were occupied by single families. As taxes and maintenance costs increased, availability of domestic help and other services decreased. At the same time, the market value of the land escalated, making private residential use doubly extravagant. Even some of the institutions that had inherited or otherwise acquired larger properties felt induced to leave; large old houses that had been used for institutional purposes were sold to redevelopers at a price high enough to allow the organization to acquire larger and more modern facilities elsewhere. A few of the mansions that had been converted into several comfortable apartments seemed able to resist economic pressures, as did some other properties, but increasingly there was reason to fear that this beautiful and historic portion of East Avenue might soon become a Bronx-like aggregation of high-rise construction.

The wringing of hands and the decrying of change, however, would not provide workable alternatives to the demolition of historic buildings and the redevelopment of their landscaped properties when they could no longer be maintained for their original purpose. Economic, political, and social interests, at all levels, were not in accord. Exceptional leadership was required, and Sterling Weaver, then president of the Landmark Society, deserves recognition here. Foreseeing potential conflict, even within his own organization, he nevertheless directed the society through several years of persuasion and negotiation, working with community and government representatives to provide a city-wide Landmark Preservation Code and to designate the East Avenue area as a preservation district, with innovative land use controls.

A complete survey of the area, containing over seven hundred buildings on hundreds of acres, was first undertaken. The New York State Council on the Arts provided assistance in this and other planning activities. Many volumes of documentation were translated into maps showing gradations of historic and architectural value, and concentrations of buildings of various types. This basic information was used to develop alternative design proposals and policy recommendations. Under the direction of Mrs. Ann Taylor, the City Planning Bureau collaborated with the Landmark Society in preparing plans and defining policy in ordinances that were adopted by the city.

21. **42 Knollwood Drive,** Pittsford. Such hand craftsmanship seems as nostalgic now as the pre-Depression optimism that is memorialized in carved wood and stone, leaded glass, and remarkable exterior plaster work, from the second decade of this century.

49

From a planning point of view, Rochester was concerned fiscally with continuing transfer of high-tax-yielding private property to tax-exempt organizations. Construction of multistory buildings might balance churches, museums, and other institutions used by the public. Furthermore, the city (with rather tightly drawn city limits) sought to bring more residents back from the suburbs. The immediate willingness of developers to erect new construction could not be disregarded.

Previous zoning had been well intended, but proved to be misguided. A height restriction had resulted in many walk-up apartments. The prevailing six-floor limit proved to be uneconomical for fireproof structures with elevators. Lower walk-up buildings (some perhaps "tax-payers") usually were lighter in construction, smaller and meaner in quality than the mansions they replaced. Ground coverage of low buildings and parking lots threatened to destroy the park-like quality of the neighborhood. Smallness itself was not necessarily a virtue; one proposal for a shoe-box-type professional building, to be inserted between much larger neighboring mansions, clearly was inappropriate. A general principle became apparent; if new construction were necessary, it would be preferable to have a few considerably taller buildings, to provide more open space and less visual obstruction of the neighborhood at eye level. Furthermore, a few high buildings, especially if set back in the interior of the large blocks, might satisfy and stabilize the market demand for rentals in the area. This would be preferable to many more lower build-

22. **Temple Sinai,** 363 Penfield Road, Brighton. The continuing vitality of the East Avenue area is expressed by this distinctive structure of earth-formed, precast panels. The wooded site has been carefully preserved, and the trees combine with an exterior, symbolic sculptural element to create the effective wall of the interior space.

51

23. Stone-Tolan House, 2370 East Avenue, Brighton. This frontier farmhouse, although one of the oldest buildings remaining in the county, reflects a concern for architectural refinement (note the wooden quoins at the corners).

24. Stone-Tolan House, 2370 East Avenue, Brighton. Careful investigation has revealed original features of this pioneer home. The large cooking fireplace and wide plank floors are characteristic of the earliest houses of the region. Perhaps more than the exterior, which does not appear so strikingly different from Colonial traditions that have continued, the interior may be recognized as a testament of the earliest settlers of Monroe County.

ings, lined along the street, replacing the historic buildings in their landscaped surroundings.

Aware of the displeasure that such a policy might cause, even to some of its own members, the Landmark Society nevertheless decided to work with change rather than against it. Since the means were not available to maintain the entire area without some new development, the objective became the best possible controlled development.

Final legislation was not drafted in a matter of months. Years of study and debate were represented in an ordinance that incorporated special incentives for the developer. He would be rewarded for respecting the historic and visual qualities of the neighborhood. By placing new construction back from the normal building line, allowing preservation of a designated historic structure, more might be built on the property, yielding more return, than possible under conventional planning restrictions. Maintenance of a consistent domestic scale in the foreground was a first concern. Appropriate limits for ultimate development were determined, from visual as well as functional considerations. It was hoped to make preservation more profitable than demolition and reconstruction.

Shortly after the new district legislation was enacted, one of the historic properties was sold. It was especially gratifying that the building was not demolished for new construction, as had been feared, but was renovated for office use. As a long-term investment the property also allowed further development in the rear. Both the historic house and its landscaped grounds have been preserved. One of the first houses to be seen in this section of East Avenue, it is the picturesque 1879 residence at Number 1545 (Plate 26). Its builder, W. W. Chapin, endowed his residence with that lively quality that his time termed "piquancy." With romantic natural surroundings, this property is located directly across the avenue from a large apartment building. Its spacious grounds and attractive landscaping, as well as the house itself, contribute visual relief and openness, maintaining the residential scale and

54

25. First Unitarian Church, 220 South Winton Road, Rochester. One of two neighboring buildings by prominent American architects of our own time, this church designed by Louis I. Kahn combines with Temple Beth El, across the street, to form an important grouping. Both brick buildings are expressively sculptural, but each evidences the distinctive manner of its designer.

character on this portion of the avenue, where many larger new developments have appeared.

This precedent may suggest to other developers the worth of historic properties, consistent with profitable development. It is, after all, the special quality of East Avenue that has created the market for tenancy here. If the fine old houses, with their lawns and trees, should disappear, the value of all investments here would decline. Planning for conservation of historic and scenic quality may preserve economic as well as cultural values.

Trees are a special glory of East Avenue. One perhaps ninety to ninety-five years old is seen across the street, in front of the apartment building at Number 1600 (Plate 27). The retention of this great beech tree has greatly enhanced the project as well as the environs.

This portion of the East Avenue neighborhood is bounded on University Avenue, only one short block to the north, by industry. This developed along a railroad line there and resulted in an exceptional model of harmonious integration. A factory well related to a residential neighborhood is the large Gleason Works (Plate 28). It was built about 1910 for the manufacture of gear-cutting machines and has been admirably maintained, with well-tended grounds complementing a neoclassical entrance facade.

Another somewhat earlier precedent for preservation through adaptive use is the professional building at 1501 East Avenue. The neo-Tudor house was built in 1913 by Henry M. Stern, with Herbert Stern as his architect. Today it appears from the avenue much as it has for some sixty years,

26. W. W. Chapin House, 1545 East Avenue, Rochester. The taste of 1879 is characterized by this picturesque residence. It was romantically sited on grounds with a winding stream and bridge. This rural scene is only a block from the

sort of industry that made it possible. Sympathetic adaptive use as offices has maintained the charm of house and grounds, affording a park-like view for a large apartment building across the avenue.

27. 1600 East Avenue, Rochester. This magnificent beech tree, perhaps ninety to ninety-five years old, upstages the apartment building in the background. Splendid trees such as this one contribute to the beauty of East Avenue and recall the importance of commercial nurseries in the nineteenth-century development of the community.

28. Gleason Works, 1000 University Avenue, Rochester. Only a block from East Avenue, this handsome building, with well-tended grounds, is an example of the effective integration of an industrial structure into a residential area.

although a large addition has been inconspicuously added to the rear. Well-established landscaping conceals changes.

Nearby, at Number 1399, is the large pink house built in the Italianate style in 1856 by Colonel Thomas C. Bates (Plate 29). A wing added in 1875 made this the largest house of that time on the avenue. It is one of few major buildings of Italianate style in the East Avenue Preservation District. Spacious grounds contribute valuably to the scenic quality of the area, particularly since generally continuous high-rise construction has extended on the other side of the street this far from Winton Road. For this reason as well as for the intrinsic historic and architectural worth of the house, its preservation is critical. When the beautifully finished and furnished interiors (with a notable music room of French period decor) were badly damaged by fire in recent years, the owner faced the difficult decision of either restoring the property or yielding to the sort of development that was beginning to surround it. Fortunately for the community and future generations, Miss Helen Ryder decided to restore the historic house to its original condition and to give it to the Landmark Society. She continues to reside here and to maintain the property, and its future protection is assured.

Shortly beyond, East Avenue is crossed by East Boulevard, which extends one block on either side of the avenue. Both of these small blocks should be visited, as each contains an outstanding landmark. On one side of the avenue is an excellent Federal building from the earliest period; on the other is a pioneer work by a famous modern architect.

Turning first to the right, at Number 70 is the Oliver Culver Tavern (Plate 30). Built in 1816 on a nearby corner of East Avenue, it was moved here in 1906. The combination of public inn and private residence was not uncommon in the frontier period, when more developed hostelries were infrequently found. The type of side door seen here has become popularly known as a "funeral door," from the notion that a coffin might be moved into and out of a front parlor through such a door. Associated with homes that also

29. Bates-Ryder House, 1399 East Avenue, Rochester. An Italian villa, as it was envisioned in its own time, this mansion, with characteristic low pitched roofs (here concealed by a balustrade), broad overhanging eaves, arched windows, and square tower, is the principal model of its kind in Monroe County as well as in the East Avenue Preservation District. The building and its extensive grounds have been given to the Landmark Society by Miss Helen Ryder.

30. Oliver Culver Tavern, 70 East Boulevard, Rochester. This splendid Federal house is the first of a remarkable pair of buildings on East Boulevard. Built originally as a tavern, it has the side door often found on such early inns. The quality of its architectural detail is evidenced by the fully developed cornice and the exceptional entrance porch. Delicacy and elegance of design mark one of the most valuable Federal houses of the region.

served as taverns, it functioned as a separate entrance to a public room. Inside there is a ballroom extending the full width of the second floor across the front. This recalls the general form of the ballroom in the Phoenix Hotel, Pittsford. It has a coved ceiling, a pair of fireplaces, and a double-floor system designed to absorb the noise and prevent the cracking of plaster ceilings below on especially festive occasions. The architectural detail of the interior is very fine, as is the development of the exterior cornice and the singular entrance porch. The property has been beautifully maintained and decorated by Miss Elizabeth Holahan, who is widely known as an authority on the restoration of period interiors. One of the parlors has been portrayed in *One Hundred Most Beautiful Rooms in America* (Helen Comstock, Viking Press, 1958).

On East Boulevard, across East Avenue, one may be surprised to discover at Number 16 a very different kind of house (Plates 31 and 32). How unusual it must have looked when it was built in 1907–8. An early work of Frank Lloyd Wright, it was the easternmost example of his "Prairie style" when built. The young Chicago architect, just beginning to attain his worldwide reputation, was commissioned by Edward Boynton. This Rochester resident was associated in the lantern business with Warren McArthur of Kenwood, Illinois, for whom Wright had designed a house built fifteen years earlier, at the beginning of the architect's career. McArthur had been one of the earliest supporters of the controversial designer. His appreciation came to be shared by the Boyntons, particularly the client's daughter, Beulah Boynton, who recalled in the *Rochester Times Union*, April 1959:

> I heard one woman tell another that my father wanted to build it for his daughter and she's a little queer.
> We particularly liked the sense of space and light in the house. There were no features about it we didn't like, or found inconvenient.
> The carpets were woven to measure in Scotland. The furniture was made after plans by Mr. Wright. The general colors were brown, cream and yellow.

Even the hardware was made to order—the window pieces, door knobs and curtain pulls. Bed linens were made for us in Ireland. Curtains were alike in every room.

I think the cost of the house was between $45,000 and $50,000. There are now three other houses on what was the original lot. The porch was originally open, now it's glassed in.

People thought it was revolutionary, and the most frequent comment I heard was that it was a style of architecture that wouldn't last.

The house is remarkably fresh sixty-five years later, and it still appears modern. Although the sale of adjoining property and the construction of larger neighboring buildings has made the house look slightly cramped, the expansive breadth of Wright's design is nevertheless apparent. This is not a large house, but continuous horizontal lines and broad overhanging eaves belie its size. One of the treasures of Monroe County is the dining room of the Boynton House (Plate 32), with the original furniture, carpet, lighting fixtures, and hardware designed by Wright.

In Monroe County, as elsewhere, Wright became a legend. George T. Swan, the son of the building's contractor, recalled, in the same newspaper article cited above:

> He [Wright] might come into town on a train that arrived at midnight. . . . He wouldn't put up at a hotel. He would hire a hack and go directly to the Boynton house and stay there the remainder of the night. He would never leave the house during his stay in Rochester, which might continue two or three

31. Edward Boynton House, 16 East Boulevard, Rochester. The second of the valuable pair of historic buildings on East Boulevard, this house is a striking contrast to the Oliver Culver Tavern, built almost a century earlier. An early work of Frank Lloyd Wright, built in 1907–8, it illustrates the dramatic and

innovative ideas of the modern master, clearly expressed in separated planes and volumes, with a pronounced linearity suggesting Japanese influences. The floating quality is characteristic of Wright's work, as is the rich development of a personal ornament in the leaded glass windows.

days. He was on the job night and day, though of course no workmen were there at night.

He once made one of his unexpected visits during a spell of miserable weather. It was cold and rainy. As yet there was no roof on the house. Wright had workmen throw up a sort of lean-to, a few two-by-fours with a tarpaulin flung over it, and he remained in this during the night. He seemed to feel that when he was here he had to live, uninterruptedly, with his work.

During one particular cold and rainy spell, my mother cooked a hot dinner and had it sent to Wright in containers that would keep the food hot. . . . Wright returned the food with thanks. He was well provided for, he said; he had a bag of raw carrots. Like the late Claude Bragdon, also of the avant-garde among architects, and for many years the leading architect in Rochester, Wright avoided meat . . . my father said that Wright was one of the most interesting men he had ever met. I wish I had been old enough to have appreciated him.

He became, in time, a kind of legend in our house. Wright, of course, was a genius, and as eccentric as most geniuses probably are.

Title to the Boynton House was acquired in 1968 by the Landmark Society. In a manner similar to other examples mentioned, it was decided that the house ought to be lived in, continuing the purpose for which it was designed. Protection was assured by restrictive covenants in the deed.

Other attractive houses are seen in this block of East Boulevard. Number 35, for example, is by the well-known architect Claude Bragdon, and was built in 1913.

32. **Edward Boynton House,** 16 East Boulevard, Rochester. The strongly linear character and the clear definition of masses and volumes are apparent on the interior as well as the exterior of the Boynton House. This valuable room retains original furnishings designed by Wright, including carpet and hardware. The large dining table incorporates combination lighting fixtures and planters on

the pedestals. The overhead lighting fixture includes some of the characteristic stained glass that appears in the windows. This important work was acquired by the Landmark Society and was resold with restrictive covenants assuring its preservation.

33. Douglas Road, Rochester. One of the comfortable side streets off East Avenue, Douglas Road still conveys a sense of well-being associated with the early twentieth century. The fine houses, generally of a 1920 character, are integrated into a cohesive neighborhood by continuous lawns and attractive landscaping.

68

Instead of retracing steps, a return to East Avenue may be made by way of Douglas Road (Plate 33), as suggested by the map. Of the many neighborhood groups of buildings and gardens in the county pointed out here, this is one of the most attractive and serves as an example of how an assemblage of buildings, good enough in themselves, can attain even greater value by becoming parts of a whole. The character of Douglas Road again recalls the 1920s, and this area is as inviting and livable a place now as it was some half-century ago. Of course, it is still an expensive neighborhood, compared to many more modest areas to be seen, but similar to them it evidences the lasting value of good design tended with loving care.

Returning to East Avenue, one sees the large William E. Sloan House at Number 1250. This brick building on broad lawns is another work of the Rochester architect Claude Bragdon and dates from 1906. Another distinctive East Avenue residence is the urban home of the architect Herbert Stern. This elegant town house at 2 Brunswick Street was built in 1922. On the southwest corner is the Jesse W. Lindsay House of 1892, by J. Foster Warner. This represents the changing tastes at the time of the Chicago World's Fair, which revived admiration of the classical—an influence evident in the works of many subsequent decades on East Avenue. For its early date, the Lindsay House was avant-garde.

J. Foster Warner was one of the most important Rochester architects, and many examples of his work may be seen, as well as that of his father, Andrew Jackson Warner, the foremost local architect of his own generation. The great stone mansion of Wilson Soule at Number 1050 (Plates 34 and 35) is also by J. Foster Warner.

Although it dates from the same year as the house previously seen, the Soule House presents a different, earlier taste more associated with the 1880s. The influence of the great American architect H. H. Richardson, and his contemporaries is apparent. The use of stone in this massive manner, together with large roofs and vigorously modeled forms recalls many buildings of the 1880s built throughout the country. Although some recollections of the Romanesque are evident, these works more fully represent a native tradition of inventive planning, appreciation of natural materials, and a certain propensity for bombast, which may be regarded as more typical of nineteenth-century America. Some scholars have seen in buildings such as this antecedents for the creative volumetric explorations of Frank Lloyd Wright, tracing influences through his mentor, Louis Sullivan, to Richardson. Certainly this is one of the major works of the local architect J. Foster Warner. It is, moreover, one of the finest houses ever built in Monroe County. Inside and out it is detailed with care and skill. The stone carving of the entrance frame is notable, as is embossed copper work under the eaves and elsewhere about the roof. On the interior, large rooms have received finely carved woodwork. The most remarkable interior feature is the Teak Room (Plate 35). An oriental fantasy of this sort often was incorporated into large and richly finished houses of the period. The room is well preserved, especially considering its fragility and age.

After the death of Wilson Soule in 1894, the house was purchased by George Eastman, who lived here with his mother until his new mansion was completed in 1905. More recently the house was acquired by the neighboring Asbury Methodist Church. The building was to have been demolished in order to allow expansion of the church facilities. However, recognizing the quality

34. **Wilson Soule House,** 1050 East Avenue, Rochester. Imposing in size, substantially built, and enriched by superior craftsmanship in the finest materials available, this mansion represents a high standard of architectural design in the 1880s. Thereafter a wave of neoclassicism swept the country, effected largely by the Chicago World's Fair. This earlier work is characterized by irregularly composed

masses of naturally expressed materials rather than by formal symmetry and classical detail. Although it derives from the Richardsonian Romanesque, it seems almost modern in some ways, recalling Louis Sullivan's prophecy at the time that the neoclassical influence of Chicago's Fair would greatly impair the development of a native architectural tradition from roots such as these.

of the mansion, many members of the congregation protested, and the loss of this major work was averted. Today it is used by the church for smaller group meetings and administrative offices.

Like East Boulevard and Douglas Road, there are many other charming side streets off East Avenue. In fact, most of the historic neighborhood is comprised of such streets. Not all of them are grand; some have always been lined with workingmen's homes. Rundel Park is noted for its malls, and Arnold Park is marked by stone gateposts. The visitor might detour around the block to see Portsmouth Terrace and Merriman Street, as suggested by the map.

The fine copper beech tree in front of the house at Number 1005 East Avenue was planted in 1870. The house itself was built five years earlier in the Italianate style. The interiors were altered in later years by J. Foster Warner and others, and they represent the best work of their periods. This property is perhaps best known for the Spencer Gardens (Plate 36), which are outstanding from aspects both of horticulture and of design. One flower, among many others, was the special subject of the late Mrs. Spencer, who re-created here a living history of the rose. The maintenance and preservation of gardens is a particular problem, but these, which have been created and cared for with so much devotion over many years, should be regarded as one of the exceptional accomplishments of a community well known for its parks, gardens, and nurseries.

35. **Wilson Soule House,** 1050 East Avenue, Rochester. An exotic oriental nook was fashionable for mansions of the late nineteenth century. The Teak Room certainly is the most remarkable feature of the interior, combining delicately carved woodwork with oriental scenes painted in sepia on canvas panels and a ceiling of gold filigree applied to red fabric.

Perhaps the closest thing Monroe County has to what the English would call a "stately home" is the great mansion at 900 East Avenue, which rivals churches and public buildings in grandeur (Plate 37). Truly baronial, it was completed in 1905 as the residence of George Eastman, the founder of Eastman Kodak Company. Just as this industry has been basic to the economy of the county, so this great house has appropriately become one of its foremost cultural monuments. A National Historic Landmark, it is now a famous museum of photography, retaining some of the principal rooms with their original furnishings, including paintings, largely of the English schools. The building was designed by the famous New York architectural firm of McKim, Mead and White in association with J. Foster Warner. In 1917 a garden loggia designed by Claude Bragdon was built on the east side of the house, and in 1919 the rear portion of the house was moved in order to enlarge the music room, which contains an organ, an instrument of which Eastman, a great patron of music, was especially fond.

George Eastman lived as a bachelor in this vast house, although he entertained regularly. He died in 1932, and in 1949 the house was opened as a museum. His birthplace, a small frame Greek Revival house, has been moved to the property, and the Dryden Theater (T. W. Moore, architect) was built here in 1950 by the Dryden family as a memorial to George Eastman, who is well remembered in many other ways for great contributions to this community.

Nearby is St. Paul's Episcopal Church, in the continuing tradition of the Gothic style for liturgical work. It was built in 1897 from the design of Heims and LaFarge of New York. A good example of adaptive use is the house at Number 740, which was modified for professional offices of the local architectural firm of Waasdorp, Northrup and Kaelber. The fine interiors, originally designed by Leon Stern for whom the house was built in 1895, have been carefully retained.

The odd-looking building on the corner, at Number 727, is one of the

36. Harris-Spencer House, 1005 East Avenue, Rochester. Gardens are among the finest of Rochester's treasures. A fragment of these extensive grounds may convey something of their quality. Specializing in roses, the Spencer gardens are among the best in the county.

distinctive works of the Rochester architect Harvey Ellis (Plate 38). This structure is another example of the inventive design being done in the 1880s, prior to the Chicago World's Fair. Influences of the prominent English architect of the period, R. Norman Shaw, are apparent—the multiple bay windows, the expansive, small-paned fenestration of the stairwell, and the vaguely Northern Renaissance detail on the chimneys and elsewhere. The general composition of the building suggests Shaw's imagination as a designer, as well as his lively manner. This building, dating from 1883, is nevertheless a highly personal statement, as is most of Ellis's work. It also may be viewed as representing the advanced taste of its decade.

Another work of J. Foster Warner is seen at Number 693, a large brick and stone house built in 1901 for Colonel Henry A. Strong, now used by the Catholic Diocese as a Retreat House. It illustrates the taste of the decade following the Chicago World's Fair. One of the few Gothic Revival works in the East Avenue Preservation District is seen at Number 666. Now the Rochester Methodist Home, its restrained design by Andrew J. Warner, the father of J. Foster Warner, employs few details specifically of the style, except for characteristic steeply pitched roofs, prominent gables, and a pointed window. It was built about 1852–54 of Medina sandstone, which was salvaged from the original canal aqueduct across the Genesee River. The builder of the house, Charles F. Bissell, constructed the second aqueduct, an important engineering work.

37. **George Eastman House,** 900 East Avenue, Rochester. George Eastman's house is a monument and a museum, housing an outstanding photographic collection as well as period rooms. Stylistically, it represents the return to more "correct" historical prototypes (generally following classical, Renaissance, or eighteenth-century models) during the decade following the Chicago World's Fair. This de-

sign is Georgian in character. It indicates the influence of the East Coast architectural establishment—in this instance the major firm of McKim, Mead and White of New York. Eastman House is registered as a National Historic Landmark.

78

The Strasenburgh Planetarium of the Rochester Museum and Science Center is one of the modern landmarks of Monroe County (Plate 39). Adding to the rich diversity of East Avenue, it seems to be an appropriate contribution from our own time. Balance and continuity are important factors in a historic district, but despite the dynamic form of this building, its careful placement on the site and muted tonality make it a good neighbor. The planetarium was designed in 1968 by the architects Waasdorp, Northrup and Kaelber.

The Century Club was built in 1900 as a residence for Albert Vogt and was designed by Leon Stern. The Third Presbyterian Church on the other side of the street was built in 1893 from designs by Orlando K. Foote in the neo-Romanesque style associated with the previous decade. It may be compared to the Soule House (Plate 34).

Approaching the city center and nearing the end of the long residential stretch of East Avenue, one finds some earlier buildings. When these first mansions were constructed, the avenue was still a country road. Three large Greek Revival houses remain together here as an important group, constructed about 1840, within a few years of each other.

Woodside (Plate 40), now the headquarters-museum of the Rochester Historical Society, was planned and constructed during the years 1838–41 for Silas O. Smith by the architect-builder Alfred M. Badger. It is one of the most distinguished Greek Revival houses in Monroe County and is one of the important mansions of its kind in New York State. Although it is similar in

38. **727 East Avenue,** Rochester. This remarkable design is the work of Harvey Ellis, one of the most creative of Rochester designers. The use of diverse elements, combined into an artful composition, is characteristic of Ellis's skill and taste, as well as of the creative state of architecture in the 1880s.

form to the neighboring Pitkin and Erickson-Perkins houses, it has been less altered than these. Furthermore, some features as well as its pyramidal composition are distinctive. The glazed lantern atop the windowed cupola is functional, lighting a central stairwell.

At the house, the Rochester Historical Society offers Carl K. Hersey's paper *The Architectural Origins of Woodside,* which discusses more fully elements of the design. Generally, the plan follows a typical arrangement, with a center entrance hall and parlors on either side. On the right are double parlors, linked by a large opening; on the left the dining room replaces the rear parlor. Both the entrance hall and the double parlors on the right show plaster cornice moldings around the ceilings and a central ceiling escutcheon, which are characteristic of the mid-nineteenth century. The glass chandeliers in these rooms seem to be more consistent with the original work than does the metal ceiling fixture in the single parlor across the hall. The splendid Art Nouveau sconces in the double parlors date from the turn of the century. The metal firebox in the front double parlor is also notable.

The single parlor to the left of the entrance seems to have received, in addition to the later metal chandelier, a new ceiling and cornice moldings. Stylistically, this work appears to belong to the Georgian Revival, one of the new modes following the Chicago World's Fair. The dining room is altered little. The black marble mantelpieces in these rooms are original.

The second-floor rooms, although commodious, are simpler in detail. Much of the work is Greek Revival in character, although one of the mantelpieces may be identified as later in date, as may some cornices, built-in cabinets, and bathrooms. The latter are especially interesting because they retain early china fixtures and fittings. Note the electric lighting fixtures in the hall and the bathrooms.

Surprising and amusing is a small room found in the rear corner of the house. Perhaps dating from the time of the other alterations at the turn of the century, it is a gentlemen's smoking room, rendered in sort of a Black

39. Strasenburgh Planetarium, Rochester Museum and Science Center, 663 East Avenue, Rochester. The dynamic, curved forms of this concrete structure continue the vigorous architectural traditions of the community. Although differing completely in style, some similarity of spirit may be seen between this modern work and Harvey Ellis's nearby house of the 1880s, a modern work in its own time.

Forest Gemütlich style. Above dark wood wainscoting carved with animal reliefs, is leather wall covering decorated with patterns of metal studs. A heavy black iron chandelier and similar gas jets on the walls match the fireplace equipment and the mantel clock. The other furnishings are appropriate: rabbits carved in-the-round serve as chair finials, while metal turtles on the hearth serve as spittoons. Heavy original upholstery and draperies remain, and a bar is secreted behind a wainscot panel.

Woodside is basically a Greek Revival mansion with some later nineteenth-century enrichment; otherwise it has been modernized little. It contains a good collection of period artifacts, well maintained by the Rochester Historical Society, and it richly conveys a sense of nineteenth-century life.

Across the street is the William Pitkin House. Although probably begun after the Silas Smith House, it may be dated about 1840. Possibly, it was designed by the same Alfred Badger, or by Nehemiah Osborn, architect of the neighboring Erickson House. The interiors have been altered, and a third floor was added soon after 1900 by the architect J. Foster Warner. Nevertheless, the exterior retains its Greek Revival character, complementing the other similar houses.

Sibley Place, with a mall, is another serene enclave off the avenue. Not being a through street, it has an air of seclusion that belies its situation, so close to the heart of the city.

40. Woodside, the Silas O. Smith House, 485 East Avenue, Rochester. This Greek Revival mansion was built by a city merchant when East Avenue was still rural. It is now the headquarters-museum of the Rochester Historical Society. Its pyramidal composition culminates in a round turret atop a square cupola; similar balustrades appear at the several levels, as well as on the massive entrance porch. The heavy cornice, with wrought iron grills inserted in the frieze band, is typical of the style. The interiors are rewarding and are open to visitors.

The third of the three neighboring Greek Revival mansions is the Aaron Erickson House (Plate 41). Later known as the Perkins House, it now is the Genesee Valley Club. Originally the work of Nehemiah Osborn, it was completed in 1842. Additions and interior alterations were designed by the New York architect John du Fais, and later by Gordon and Kaelber of Rochester, with the consultation of Carl Schmidt. Although the interior of the house has been much changed, the exterior of the main portion retains its original appearance. The spacious grounds and landscaping also contribute to the quality of the area.

East Avenue continues to the commercial center of the city, which may be seen ahead. But because several blocks of little interest intervene, the visitor may prefer to turn at Prince Street. Before leaving the avenue at this point, a last house, slightly beyond, may be noted. At Number 400, on the right-hand side, is the residence built in 1868 by Hiram Sibley, president of Western Union and then the wealthiest man in Rochester. Originally the building was Italianate in style. It has since been remodeled in a neo-Georgian style; design and craftsmanship are of high quality throughout (Plate 42).

Further beyond, the end of the residential neighborhood is effectively marked by the fine Sibley and Fitch buildings of brick and stone, flanking the avenue at Alexander Street. This gateway is a model of sensitive urban design, providing not only a demarcation but also a transition. The richer in detail of these two structures was built in 1925 by Hiram Sibley as a fitting neighbor to several of the family's houses (Plate 43). The architects were Shepley, Bulfinch and Abbot of Boston.

Paralleling East Avenue, one block to the north, is University Avenue. The Gleason Works (Plate 28), previously mentioned, is located on this street. Nearer to the city center, the old campus of the University of Rochester developed on this avenue, giving it its name. Prince Street is one short block linking East Avenue with what has become an important university-museum

41. Aaron Erickson House, 421 East Avenue, Rochester. One of three important Greek Revival mansions comprising an exceptional group, this house was built in 1842 by a prosperous wool merchant. Now a private club, the landscaped grounds, with appropriate features such as brick walks and fences in the style of the original period, enhance the avenue.

42. Hiram Sibley House, 400 East Avenue, Rochester. An interior such as this conveys much about those whose leadership developed not only the commerce and industry of Monroe County but also its notable culture. This livable room was remodeled in the early twentieth century, within an older Italianate house of the Civil War era.

complex on University Avenue. On one side of Prince Street is the former Sacred Heart Academy, which fills most of the block. Built originally in 1868, it has additions dating from the 1880s, 1890s, and more recent periods. On the other side of the street, at Number 7, is a prickly frame house built in 1878 by William Cogswell and designed by John R. Thomas. Deriving remotely from the Gothic Revival, but with something of the character of Eastlake, it is an imaginative work well representing the 1870s.

Next door, at Number 9, is one of the most remarkable buildings in the county—the library wing of a house, since demolished, that was built by James S. Watson (Plate 44). The wing, added in 1903, was designed by the New York architect John du Fais, who also worked on the interiors of the nearby Genesee Valley Club (the Aaron Erickson House). It was Harvey Ellis, the talented local architect, who was responsible for the rich interiors of the Watson Library. Ellis recently had returned from the Midwest, where his special talents for architectural delineation had been employed. Although he rejoined his brother Charles for a final period of architectural practice in Rochester, Harvey was occupied primarily with painting, print making, and art instruction during this later Rochester period. The more exotic character of the interior is attributable to the man in his last years, whom Mrs. Watson is said to have recalled as "a drunkard and a genius." The design of the lavish woodwork and the painting of the ceiling are the last architectural commissions of Harvey Ellis.

Prince Street is headed, across University Avenue, by a fine grouping of important buildings around the original campus of the University of Rochester. The oldest of these is Anderson Hall (Plate 45), built in 1861, which is located at the center rear of the campus. Alexander R. Esty of Boston was the architect. This important building has been adapted for office use, but since another significant neighboring structure was recently demolished, the fate of the rest of these buildings seems uncertain. Some have been used as residences for University of Rochester students of the Eastman School of

43. Hiram Sibley Building, 311 Alexander Street, Rochester. Richly sculptural, this is one of a handsome pair of buildings flanking the avenue, built to serve as a gateway between the commercial and residential districts.

44. James S. Watson Library, 9 Prince Street, Rochester. An unexpected surprise is "The Petit Trianon," as it is known locally, after the model at Versailles. Although of brick combined with stone, this evocation of eighteenth-century France was designed by the New York architect John du Fais as the library wing of a larger house, which has disappeared. The diminutive scale and such features as its conservatory and terraces contribute to the charm of this sophisticated folly.

90

Music, which is located downtown. Certainly the grouping of the old campus as a whole is of importance and ought to be fully retained.

The most imposing feature of the old campus is the landmark tower of Cutler Union (Plate 46), designed in 1926 by the local architects Gordon and Kaelber in the idiom that has become known as "collegiate Gothic." The successors to this firm also designed the addition to the Memorial Art Gallery (Plate 46), which is situated between the Cutler Union and the handsome original gallery building, built in 1913 in neoclassical style from designs by John Gade of New York. This was a small but distinguished building, and designing a large modern addition, as well as relating it to the Cutler Union, presented a problem. Certainly the solution may be pointed to as a model of sensitive accommodation. Uncompromisingly of its own time, the new gallery wing nevertheless shows deference to its seniors on both sides. It was designed in 1968 by Waasdorp, Northrup and Kaelber of Rochester. A visit to this fine museum may be a fitting conclusion to a tour of the East Avenue area.

45. Anderson Hall, 75 College Avenue, Rochester. Of regional Medina sandstone, this mansard-roofed structure of the Civil War era remains on the original campus of the University of Rochester. Its simple dignity is evidence that not all post–Greek Revival work was notable for excess.

46. Cutler Union and **Memorial Art Gallery,** 560 and 490 University Avenue, Rochester. The "collegiate Gothic" tower of the 1926 University of Rochester building is linked visually with an older art gallery by a new wing. This is a model of a modern work that, with taste and restraint, respects important neighbors. The landscaping also is effective in integrating the several buildings, and the designer may be commended for his modesty in planting a double row of low trees in front of the new structure.

5

DOWNTOWN ROCHESTER:

From the Liberty Pole to Washington Square

The central city is oriented around two focal points. The first is the Liberty Pole, where East Avenue joins Main Street, and the principal commercial district begins. The second, several blocks down Main Street, is centered on the Genesee River and the Four Corners.

At the end of East Avenue, rising before a large, brick department store, which provides an effective backdrop, is the Liberty Pole (Plate 47). This modern sculptural work recalls an earlier historic feature found in many communities in the early nineteenth century. When a small triangular area at East Avenue and Main Street was cleared by urban renewal in 1962, a design competition resulted in the commissioning of the local architect James H. Johnson to design this 1965 equivalent to the original Liberty Pole, which had been located on the block.

Visible for a long distance up East Avenue, the imposing building of the Sibley, Lindsay & Curr Company is a handsome example of early commercial architecture (Plate 47). It was built in stages—1904, 1911, and 1926—from plans by J. Foster Warner. Large windows horizontal in proportion are set deep in a vigorously expressed structural frame, recalling the influential, late-nineteenth-century Chicago School of architecture. Few modern commercial buildings in Rochester surpass old Sibley's for clarity and effectiveness of architectonic expression. Fortunately, the building has not been modernized, as have many early commercial buildings.

To the right of the Sibley Building are the tower of St. Joseph's Roman Catholic Church and the monumental, arched entrance of the Rochester Savings Bank (Plate 48). The exterior of the bank belies the splendor of its interior. Few cathedrals of the New World evidence the grandeur of this 1928 "temple of commerce" (Plate 49). J. Foster Warner, the architect of the Sibley Building and of so many other important local works, was associated with the New York firm of McKim, Mead and White in the design of the bank, as he was for George Eastman's East Avenue mansion (Plate 37). The richness of the main banking room, with precious and richly ornamented materials and surfaces, is nevertheless restrained by a controlling taste.

The painted ceiling is the work of Ezra Winter, the American muralist, as is the great mosaic panel, inscribed, "Industry and Thrift are the Foundations of Prosperity." An angelic, winged figure of Prosperity rewards a man who holds a spade in one hand and a harvest bounty in the other, as well as a woman who supports a child on her left, her right hand grasping a treasure chest. The mosaics were produced from Winter's designs at the Ravenna Studios in Berlin, under the direction of the artist. His work also enriches Rochester's Eastman Theater, which is the work of McKim, Mead and White.

St. Joseph's Roman Catholic Church (Plate 50), in the next block of Franklin Street, is a design distinctive for its time and place. Begun in 1843 of Lockport Greystone, which is a grey form of Medina sandstone, the construction continued over several years from designs of Jones and Nevins. Little is known of this firm—even, in fact, whether they were local. The authorship of the 1909–10, neo-Renaissance tower also is unknown; certainly it is a design in its own stylistic vocabulary of considerable merit, although its rather elaborate character may obscure the simple dignity of the original work. The projecting, one-floor vestibule (unfortunately, with aluminum entrance doors) seems to deflate the grandeur of the building. One can only suppose that it is a fairly recent addition to enclose exterior steps, but the importance of this major monument ought to warrant more sensitive

47. Main Street and **Liberty Pole; Sibley, Lindsay & Curr Company,** Rochester. The Liberty Pole triangle, where East Avenue meets Main Street, is a pivotal point. A modern reconstruction of the historic pole is backed by Sibley's, a landmark of the community. This fine commercial building serves an important visual function in terminating the East Avenue gateway.

96

reconstruction. The interior evidences the same sort of distinctiveness apparent on the original portions of the exterior, employing the sort of U-shaped mezzanine gallery common in earlier meeting houses of the region, but giving expression to a newly emerging nineteenth-century character.

Nearby, as indicated on the map, is a small residential area known as the Grove Place Preservation District. This has survived as a pleasant neighborhood, remarkable for its proximity to the center of the city. On Gibbs Street is a row of 1870s town houses that has been designated a city landmark (Plate 51), as has the Ward House at Number 18 Grove Place (Plate 52). This handsome Italianate house is important not only in itself but also as a centerpiece for the surrounding preservation district. It is another example of preservation by continued use. The Ward House was deeded to the Landmark Society by the late Mrs. F. Hawley Ward. Like the Bates-Ryder House on East Avenue (Plate 29), this property required considerable work, and Mrs. Ward similarly decided to improve and will for the future rather than to abandon the property. The broad eaves were rebuilt, and the crowning roof balustrade was reconstructed. The balustrade is a distinctive feature, repeating the motif that occurs at the entrance porch. The delicate iron balconies are of similar quality, and even the windows and their shutters, like the glazed

48. **Sibley's, St. Joseph's Roman Catholic Church,** and **Rochester Savings Bank,** Liberty Pole triangle, Rochester. Diverse works of architecture, seen together from the Liberty Pole: The mercantile, religious, and commercial harmonize in a striking townscape.

front door, are uncommon. Throughout, this is an exceptionally fine example of mid-nineteenth-century taste and craftsmanship, as well as sensitive appreciation for it in our own time.

Nearby is the famous Eastman Theater and Eastman School of Music. George Eastman's love of music is suggested by the organ in his East Avenue mansion, but more so by this great institution, magnificently housed in the structures of 1922 designed by McKim, Mead and White of New York, together with the Rochester architects Gordon and Kaelber. The New York architects also contributed to the Eastman House and the Rochester Savings Bank.

The rich interiors of the Eastman Theater (Plate 53), with murals by Ezra Winter, have been recently restored as a gift to the community from the Eastman Kodak Company, continuing the original beneficence of George Eastman. Because the concert halls may not be open when one is in the neighborhood, and because it is preferable to experience these spaces filled with the activity for which they were designed, the visitor is urged to return for one of the frequent performances at the theater.

49. Rochester Savings Bank, 40 Franklin Street, Rochester. One of the most glorious interiors in Monroe County, combining glass mosaics on the walls, marble mosaics on the pavement, decoratively painted wood-coffered ceiling, and monumental Rouge Antique marble columns, this design is the work of the same collaboration of New York and Rochester architects responsible for Eastman House.

99

On returning to the Liberty Pole, one may visit Midtown Plaza (Plate 54), a modern complex across Main Street from the Sibley store. Midtown Plaza was redeveloped in the interior of a city block, incorporating most of the existing buildings on the street frontages. Although the historical precedent for covered shopping arcades is quite old, this 1962 project, designed by Victor Gruen Associates of Los Angeles, was much publicized and was influential afar as an early example of downtown regeneration. Like most American cities, the Rochester metropolitan area has seen the development of many regional shopping centers, threatening the cultural as well as the economic vitality of the downtown area. The confidence expressed by this major project, which incorporated a new hotel atop an office tower, in addition to commercial and parking facilities, was evidence of the genuine leadership of local, private enterprise. The skylighted central mall is surrounded by two levels of shops, and the enclosed pedestrian circulation links existing facilities with new ones on the block.

50. **St. Joseph's Roman Catholic Church,** 108 Franklin Street, Rochester. An important monument from the pre–Civil War era, this stone church employs structural round arches, but seems more to reflect the contemporary Greek Revival era in its simplicity and monumental scale than to characterize the coming Italianate mode, which is represented by the small building next door. The original structure of the 1840s did not have a spire and was terminated at the point indicated by the difference in stone coloration. The richly modeled steeple was constructed in the first decade of this century. The newer vestibule seems to mar the design of the main structure. The interior is distinctive, employing side galleries.

102

A bridge from the upper shopping level leads to the Xerox development on an adjoining block (Plates 55 and 56). Dominated by a dark-colored skyscraper that has become a prominent feature on the skyline, the development incorporates landscaped space. The design is the work of Welton Becket and Associates of Los Angeles. From the bridge between the two projects, one sees the Marine Midland Bank Building of 1970, designed by Skidmore, Owings and Merrill of New York (Plate 55). Known internationally, particularly for their high-rise structures, these architects have expressed the structural loading of members that make up the wall, by enlarging those carrying the greater load. The resulting undulation of the concrete exterior walls near the base of the building is a notable feature.

Also nearby may be seen the new Lincoln First Bank Building by the New York architects John Graham and Company, completed in 1973 (Plate 13). This new landmark is distinguished by white, vertical fins subtly arranged in a radial pattern so that the appearance of the tower changes dynamically as the observer moves and views it from different positions.

51. Row Houses, 128–152 Gibbs Street, Rochester. A small, quiet neighborhood only a block or so from Main Street, the Grove Place Preservation District is a convenient and attractive place to live. These row houses are of a type not common in upstate New York west of the Hudson Valley. Built in the 1870s, they still serve as a model of urban housing preferable to many alternatives available today.

In the same neighborhood, across the street from the Xerox Tower, fronting on Washington Square, is the First Universalist Church (Plate 56), the last remaining major work of Claude Bragdon. Although the prominent situation enhances the landmark quality of the Bragdon building, this very situation may make its preservation especially difficult. The migration of the congregation and the church's proximity to intensive development of highly valued property make its future uncertain.

Claude Bragdon also designed Rochester's New York Central Station, which was demolished in recent years. Several other of his public buildings and private residences remain, but the First Universalist Church must be regarded as his finest extant design. Built in 1908, the style is assured, mature, and personal, deriving indirectly from historical precedents, but synthesizing these into an attitude that recognized the twentieth century but sought to adapt a cultural heritage into new, transitional forms. Not a revolutionary, Bragdon nevertheless incorporated into a brick church, which recalls some Lombard

52. **Ward House,** 18 Grove Place, Rochester. This mid-nineteenth-century Italianate house serves as the focal point of the Grove Place Preservation District. With good ironwork and a newly reconstructed roof balustrade of unique design matching that of the entrance porch, this property was deeded to the Landmark Society, thus assuring its survival as a key element of the small downtown neighborhood.

models of northern Italy, frankly expressed iron structure, utilizing rivets for decorative effect. The furniture, designed by the architect, does not imitate historic models, but is characterized by a simple and natural design language that was Bragdon's own. Although it is not a large building, the centrally oriented interior spaces attain dignity (Plate 57). Together with its notable organ, the building and its furnishings should continue to be used.

Claude Bragdon (1866–1946) was an exceptional man. In addition to his gifts for visual imagery, his writings evidence a philosophical turn of mind. A brief but excellent biographical sketch has been written by Erville Costa ("Claude F. Bragdon, Architect, Stage Designer and Mystic," *Rochester History*, October 1967). In 1923 Bragdon left Rochester, giving up the practice of architecture in order to begin a second, equally productive career as a stage designer. Perhaps he is best remembered today for this later role, but his few remaining architectural works should not be lost or forgotten.

53. Eastman Theater, 425 East Main Street, Rochester. Rochester is known afar for several things, especially photography, flowers, and music. George Eastman, who also grew flowers, is remembered not only for Eastman Kodak but also for the Eastman School of Music. One of the leading conservatories in the country, this famous institution and its concert halls were a magnificient gift to the community and the nation.

The First Universalist Church on Washington Square is complemented, on the opposite side, by St. Mary's Roman Catholic Church, and between them the square frames a monument of Lincoln standing guard over the Civil War Soldiers' Memorial. Washington Square has become even more important to downtown Rochester, not only because of the construction of the Xerox Tower, but also because the principal arterial access to the city from the east now delivers visitors directly to this urban plaza, which serves as an introductory gateway to downtown.

The walking tour of the east side of the Genesee River ends at Washington Square. On the way to the Four Corners, the point of departure for the next chapter, one may cross the river by either the Main Street bridge or the Court Street bridge, which provides a view of the old stone aqueduct that was built to carry the Erie Canal across the river. When the canal was later filled with earth, it became Broad Street, and a road surface was built atop the aqueduct. It remains a major engineering work from the early nineteenth century and a genuine landmark of Monroe County.

54. Midtown Plaza, East Main Street and South Clinton Avenue, Rochester. Widely influential as an early and very successful model of downtown revitalization, the interior of a city block was developed atop several levels of public parking to connect existing buildings around the perimeter of the block. The central concourse has become an all-season town square.

109

55. Marine Midland Bank Building, 1 Marine Midland Plaza, Rochester; **Xerox Building,** Xerox Square, Rochester. The regeneration of downtown Rochester that began with Midtown Plaza has been continued by the erection of several towers in the surrounding blocks. Prominent on the new skyline are these buildings by two nationally known firms of architects: the Marine Midland Building of 1970 is by Skidmore, Owings and Merrill of New York; the Xerox Building of 1968, appearing to the left, is by Welton Becket and Associates of Los Angeles.

56. Washington Square: First Universalist Church, Court Street and South Clinton Avenue, Rochester; **Xerox Building,** Xerox Square, Rochester. The most important remaining work of Claude Bragdon, a prominent local architect who went on to greater fame as a New York theatrical designer, this church is dramatically contrasted with its neighboring tower, the Xerox Building. A prominent location on a downtown square enhances the landmark quality of the church, but like many other urban churches, changing patterns of population and land use have made the future of this landmark uncertain.

111

112

Between the old aqueduct and the Court Street bridge is the Rundel Memorial Building of the Rochester Public Library. A structure of the 1930s modernistic style, it is notable especially for its construction across an overflow from an old mill race, which may be seen from the riverside. From the Court Street bridge, looking south, one can see, on the west bank of the river, the Lehigh Valley Railroad depot, now boarded up, awaiting adaptive use.

57. First Universalist Church, Court Street and South Clinton Avenue, Rochester. The effective spatial composition of the interior is enhanced by furniture and even lighting fixtures designed by Claude Bragdon. Although his greater fame derived from theatrical design, his architecture is not superficially decorative; it integrates thoughtful proportions and spacial relationships, with appreciation for modern as well as traditional materials and techniques. The steel structure overhead is exposed, making decorative use of rivet heads.

6

The Genesee River and Four Corners

Main Street, extending westward from the Liberty Pole, declines slightly for a few blocks and then crosses the Genesee River. At one time buildings bridged the river on both sides of the street, so that the water was not visible. In recent years, however, there has been considerable clearance in this quarter. While some good buildings have been lost, some new construction of architectural quality has appeared.

At the Four Corners, one of the most memorable features of Rochester and Monroe County is the remarkable Powers Building (Plates 58–62, and 63). Situated at Main and State streets, it is a landmark in the truest sense. In addition to its visual prominence, it evidences a historical process of change, having grown in stages as the city and its commerce expanded.

The appearance of the first portion of the Powers Building, immediately following the Civil War, may be regarded as an expression of optimism and a glorification of commerce. Unlike some of our speculative buildings today, the Powers Block was not meanly conceived. The design derives from Second Empire fashions of the era, characterized by attenuated vertical proportions and mansard roof, with bracketed cornice and metal cresting. The elaborate dormers are consistent with this French style. Stone walls incised with small-scaled carving reduce the visual solidity of the five stories of masonry. (The side additions to the building are well-known examples of cast iron construction.) Rows of windows alternate full and flattened arches, and the horizontal entablatures at every floor level contrast with the otherwise vertical proportions. Both the arched windows and the pronounced horizontal

58. Powers Building, 16 West Main Street, Rochester. Growth and change: The evolution of a landmark is recorded in these illustrations. One of the unique features of the county, the remarkable Powers Block has expanded with the fortunes of the community. This view shows the original portion a year after its construction in 1869. To the left, an addition already is being constructed.

banding suggest the Italianate mode. In 1869 the new building must have seemed very fresh, very sophisticated, and very European. The architect was Andrew Jackson Warner, who drew the plans for Daniel Powers, a nineteenth-century Rochester man of wealth, and patron of the arts.

The interiors of the building also are interesting (Plates 61 and 62). The Powers Block has been recorded for the Historic American Buildings Survey and is listed on the National Register of Historic Places. One of the most eccentric but lovable elements of the urban townscape, this rare commercial building is one of the best of its kind and should continue to be a prominent feature of the Rochester scene.

The imposing Classical Revival bank building next to the Powers Block on State Street is a good example of the historicism prevalent in the early twentieth century, when certain archaic styles were considered appropriate to certain building types. Although in retrospect this period may appear to have been a dead end in terms of cultural consequences, the inherent quality of both the design and the execution of such buildings needs to be recognized, as well as the practical fact that buildings such as these will never be seen again, due to basic changes in the society, its resources and economy. The First National Bank, formerly the Monroe County Savings Bank, was built in 1924 from the design of Mowbray and Uffinger. It may be observed from the local evidence that in the 1920s there occurred a remarkable flowering of buildings rich in material, craftsmanship, and design.

It was nearly a half-century later before another era of significant commercial building occurred. Midtown Plaza initiated the construction of a series of important new works in the 1960s in downtown Rochester. Across State Street from the century-old Powers Block is one of the more recent of these structures: the Crossroads Building (Plate 63), a handsome, new, dark-hued office tower designed by Kahn and Jacobs of New York. Constructed in 1969 on land cleared for urban renewal, this building, housing the Security Trust Company, has replaced some good, old buildings lost in the process;

59. Powers Building, 16 West Main Street, Rochester. The addition to the left has been completed, a second tier of mansard roof has been added, and these stories have been extended over the adjoining building on the right. The beginnings of a tower appear, which was to grow even more prominently on the Rochester skyline.

but, in the balance, the new work, which has received notice nationally, is a gain for the community.

On a third corner of the Four Corners is the Wilder Building (Plate 63), another important commercial structure. It was the tallest in the city when built in 1888, surpassing even the tower of the Powers Block, until the latter was raised still higher to outdo its new competition. The architects of the brick skyscraper, one of the first of its kind, were Andrew J. Warner and William Brockett. A. J. Warner had been the designer, some twenty years earlier, of the Powers Building, diagonally across from the Four Corners intersection.

The significance of the Wilder Building may not be apparent today, but one must appreciate it in the context of the 1880s, remembering that it was this decade that saw the emergence of the modern skyscraper. New construction methods were required, and without the elevator, such tall buildings would not have been usable. But widespread use of elevators had to await replacement of hydraulic by electrical equipment, not introduced until after the Wilder Building was constructed. The Wilder Building, still wearing the fashions of the 1880s, dates from the last year of that decade and forecasts

60. Powers Building, 16 West Main Street, Rochester. The Powers Block in its final form: still a third tier of mansard roof has been added, wedding-cake style, and the tower raised by several floors. This allowed the Powers Block to top the height of newer buildings and to remain for five more years the tallest point on the skyline.

the changes of the next. It is truly a pioneer building of its type, a monument to the audacity of its time and its builders. Certainly it must have been a triumph for A. J. Warner, then approaching the end of his outstanding, early professional career. His son would carry forward advanced design ideas for commercial buildings with the great Sibley store of 1904.

Stylistically the Wilder Building represents the Richardsonian style of the 1880s, which is more apparent in the rougher masonry on the ground floor than it is in the brick on the upper floors. Of course, even Richardson himself could not reconcile the contradiction of a neo-Romanesque sky-scraper. The arches and the decorative turrets at the corners and above the entrance are reminiscent of distant stylistic origins. Originally the four cor-ners of the building were surmounted with pinnacles, as were the turrets above the entrance. Further discussion of the technical achievement of this structure for its time is found in an unpublished paper by Lee S. Kimbrough entitled "The Importance of the Wilder Building, the German Insurance Building, and the Ellwanger and Barry Building in the Development of Skeletal Construction in the United States" (University of Rochester, 1964).

61. Powers Building, 16 West Main Street, Rochester. The period character of the exterior is also retained on the interior. Spatial drama is combined with excellent detail.

121

A short distance from the Four Corners, as shown on the map, is the old Federal Building, at Church and Fitzhugh streets (Plates 64 and 65). This is a major work of the Rochester architect Harvey Ellis. Built between 1885 and 1889, it again shows the influence in that decade of Richardson's neo-Romanesque style. There is a simliarity to other buildings of the 1880s that have been seen previously, such as the Wilson Soule House (Plates 34 and 35) and the Third Presbyterian Church on East Avenue. In this instance the talented hand of Harvey Ellis appears throughout, although he worked in partnership with his brother, Charles. The well-known talents of Harvey as an artist have suggested that he was principally responsible for the designs resulting from their partnership. Claude Bragdon, who had worked for Charles Ellis, recalled that Harvey's brother was generally occupied in getting the work and left its execution to others. Harvey practiced with his brother between 1879 and 1885, went to the Midwest to work with several firms there, and returned to Rochester a decade later. His drawings from the Midwest sojourn earned him a wide reputation. As mentioned previously, the Watson Library was the only known architectural work from his final period in Rochester; the Federal Building from the earlier period certainly represents

62. **Powers Building,** 16 West Main Street, Rochester. The open stairways, with balusters and treads of metal contrasting with black and white marble pavements, are spectacular from many points of view.

his major accomplishment here. A source of further information on this talented and interesting personality is a paper by Mary Elizabeth Lipscomb, prepared at the Department of Fine Arts, University of Rochester, 1969. An illustrated monograph also is available from the Memorial Art Gallery, with contributions by Jean R. France, Howard S. Merritt, Blake McKelvey, and Roger G. Kennedy.

From the Four Corners intersection, en route to the historic Third Ward, one may walk through several important downtown buildings. The Monroe County Courthouse (now the County Office Building) appears a short distance to the west, on Main Street (Plates 66 and 68). Built between 1894 and 1896, it represents the neoclassic revival of that decade. Here the model is drawn from the Italian Renaissance rather than from the antique, and it is different in kind from the classicism of the Greek Revival. The studied design and careful detailing of the facade as well as of the interiors indicate high standards of a period that has not always been admired for its taste. Built of New Hampshire granite, this monument is another major work of J. Foster Warner, the local architect whose work is seen so frequently here, and the son of the architect of the Powers and Wilder buildings. One may walk through

63. Four Corners, Main, State, and Exchange streets, Rochester. Another pivotal point, like the Liberty Pole up Main Street, is the intersection near the Genesee River where important commercial buildings, dating from the Civil War era to the present, are located. On the left is the Crossroads Building of 1969; in the center is the Wilder Building of 1888; the Powers Building on the right is a century older than its counterpart across the street.

the courthouse, see its imposing interior, and emerge from the rear between the courthouse and the City Hall, fronted across Fitzhugh Street by another pair of valuable buildings.

This group of four historic structures on Fitzhugh Street is one of the most important in the county (Plates 67 and 68). Two are governmental, the County Courthouse and the City Hall; one is educational, the Rochester Free Academy; and the fourth is religious, St. Luke's Episcopal Church. The Erie Canal once passed by this group, where Broad Street is now located. The oldest of the buildings, St. Luke's was built concurrent with the canal, dating from 1824 (Plates 67 and 69). This Episcopal church, designed by Josiah R. Brady, is a remarkably early example of nineteenth-century Gothic Revival. St. Luke's has been illustrated (*Journal of the Society of Architectural Historians,* March 1966) as a possible influence on the design of the oldest church in Cleveland, Ohio, built a decade later. The architect of the Cleveland church migrated from Rochester several years after the construction of St. Luke's; it is not known whether he was in any way associated with the construction of Brady's church here. Josiah Brady was a New York architect

64. **Old Federal Building,** Church and North Fitzhugh streets, Rochester. Another work of the 1880s in the neo-Romanesque style popularized by the American architect H. H. Richardson, this is the major work of the prominent local designer Harvey Ellis. A genuine landmark, it presents a special problem of preservation since it no longer serves its original purpose. Like urban churches, old government buildings present immediate problem of adaptive use.

remembered for an early Greek Revival example there, the Second Trinity Church.

Limestone quarried at Auburn, New York, was used in the construction of St. Luke's (brick and wood were the more common building materials used in Rochester at that time). It is basically a simple rectangular building, with pedimented roof of classical proportions, with a square tower like that found on churches of the Federal and earlier Colonial periods, deriving from the English Georgian mode. Even contrasting stone quoins at the corner recall this tradition. The employment of pointed arches for windows seems to be one of the few suggestions of the Gothic, but the rather sophisticated window openings at the lower stages of the tower indicate an attempt to recapture the spirit of the medieval style.

The wood Gothic belfry seems to be wedded slightly incongruously to the stone tower. In fact, an illustration from an old Rochester newspaper, the *GEM*, dated 22 January 1931, shows what appears to be the original arrangement of the top stage of the tower; instead of the wood belfry with its crocketed gables on four sides, the drawing shows a square-topped element, similar

65. Old Federal Building, Church and North Fitzhugh streets, Rochester. The arcaded interior courts of the Federal Building and the Monroe County Courthouse are similar expressions of civic pride, although one represents a style of the 1880s, deriving remotely from the Romanesque, and the other the taste of the 1890s, emulating the Renaissance.

129

to the lower stages; and the material appears to be stone, surrounding a pointed arch less vertical in proportion than those employed elsewhere. Similarly, there were four corner pinnacles (each having a weathervane) with crenellations between them. Otherwise, the exterior of St. Luke's was changed little in nearly a century and a half. The interior of this historic building retains a pre–Civil War character (Plate 69). Alterations resulting from the installation of an organ in 1966 were accompanied by careful chancel restoration, advised by Professor Harley J. McKee of Syracuse University.

The Rochester Free Academy next door (Plate 67), now the Board of Education, is a major work of Andrew J. Warner, the father of the architect of the Monroe County Courthouse. The Free Academy is a highly sophisticated, elegantly crafted work dating from 1872–73. Similar to some of the best work of the time in England, there is a decorative surface quality, largely flat, expressing frank use of brick, enriched with flush bands of stone and elaborately emphasized pointed arches over the openings. The contrast of plain surface with delicately carved colonnettes and incised panels above the window transoms, the important slate roofs, and the lively, if somewhat agitated, angularity are intrinsically consistent with a stylistic whole, well understood and well expressed here. Certainly the Rochester Free Academy is one of A. J. Warner's major accomplishments and the best building of its

66. Monroe County Courthouse, 39 West Main Street, Rochester. These serene arcades, opulent in material and detail, express the romanticized classicism of the time. It is not difficult to see why such images were welcomed in the 1890s at the time of the Chicago World's Fair.

kind in the county. These two adjoining buildings, the church and the school, tell something of a sophisticated design movement in England that greatly affected this country as well. St. Luke's is an Episcopal church, appropriately, for it was a liturgical movement in the English church that actively promoted a return to Gothic models in the United States as elsewhere. At this early date, St. Luke's was not the "correct" sort of church that would have been approved later in the century, when the Gothic was better understood. A. J. Warner's Rochester Free Academy, next door, shows a half-century's development of the style.

67. St. Luke's Episcopal Church and **Rochester Free Academy,** 17 and 13 South Fitzhugh Street, Rochester. This pair of important historic structures, together with the courthouse and City Hall across the street, comprises one of the most important groupings in the county. The church and the school (now Board of Education offices) represent early and later phases of the Gothic Revival in the nineteenth century. In 1824 St. Luke's Church was built beside the new Erie Canal. In form it is basically a meeting house of the Federal style. The use of stone, however, sets it apart from typical models of the period, and the Gothic elements, although only decorative, made this church distinctive at a time when Federal buildings such as the Phoenix Hotel in Pittsford (Plate 14) were still new. The academy, in contrast to the church, is a sophisticated work a half-century later, showing awareness of stylistic trends in Victorian England.

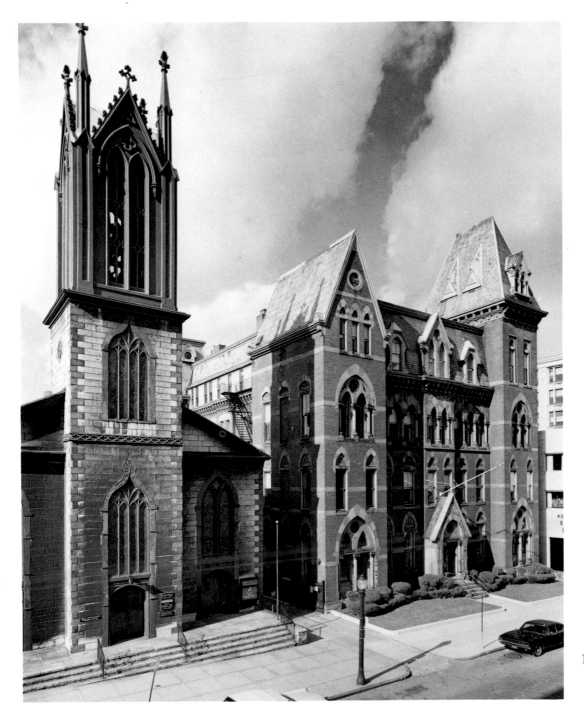

133

134

Across the street, next to his son's courthouse, is A. J. Warner's City Hall (Plate 68), dating from 1874–75. Here the elder Warner used Lockport Greystone for the design, employing contrasting cut stone in a manner similar to that of the Rochester Free Academy, although with less adherence to the Ruskinesque Gothic model. There seems to be less homage here to historical influence, and more self-reliance. The City Hall is a linear and lively building of the 1870s, not yet representing the rotund, neo-Romanesque stone style of Richardson, identified more with the next decade. Like the Gothic academy, the City Hall is characterized by angularity and pronounced verticality, but there is a prevailing restraint and a contentment with the simple repetition of similar elements. This seems fresh today, as does its expression of natural materials.

68. Monroe County Courthouse, 39 West Main Street; **City Hall,** 30 Broad Street, Rochester. These buildings are part of the grouping of four historic structures on Fitzhugh Street. The four buildings vary in age, type, and style. They represent the three-quarters of a century between the completion of the Erie Canal (which now is Broad Street, in the foreground of the photograph) and the time of the Chicago World's Fair, recalled by the courthouse of the 1890s.

To appreciate the varied inheritance from these decades, we should try to view the works as they were seen in their own time. Most architects in any era approach a new commission as an opportunity to do the best of which they are capable, and each generation leaves behind what it considers to be best representative of its capabilities.

69. St. Luke's Episcopal Church, 17 South Fitzhugh Street, Rochester. A remarkable chancel terminates the Gothic meeting house of 1824. Introduced at varying times between 1836 and 1844, the chancel furniture, rising in tiers of rich woodwork with integral lighting fixtures, is among the treasures of the region. The decorative, painted plaster work of the chancel has been restored from a pre–Civil War design found in old photographs.

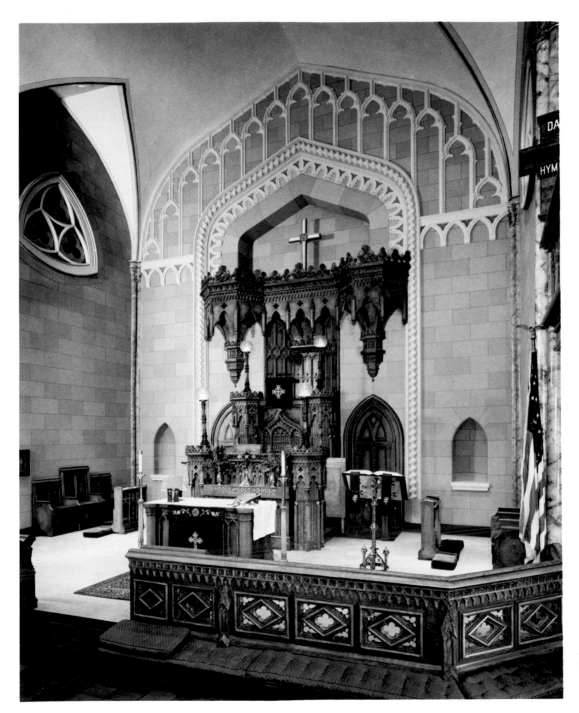

7

THE THIRD WARD

Once Rochester's finest residential neighborhood, before the East Avenue or Mount Hope areas were much developed, the Third Ward suffered greatly from neglect and demolition in more recent times. Nevertheless, continuing deterioration has been averted dramatically, at a time when even some who were sympathetic to reclamation believed it was too late.

The Erie Canal separated St. Luke's Episcopal Church on Fitzhugh Street from the Third Ward. Close to the center of town, the elegant neighborhood continued for generations as a genteel place to live. Gradually, however, as older residents disappeared, many larger houses were adapted to multifamily use. Absentee owners sometimes did not maintain properties as well as had resident owners, nor did new tenants always develop an identification with the neighborhood or a sense of responsibility for it. The Rochester Institute of Technology used some of the old structures, perhaps saving a few, but demolishing others of value. Deterioration had advanced, with accompanying social and economic problems, when demolition of much of the old Third Ward was proposed under an Urban Renewal Program.

The Landmark Society owned a key structure that was not directly threatened by renewal; it was situated on the very edge of the district, as it had been defined by modern arterial highway boundaries. The Campbell-Whittlesey House (Plates 77–79) had been the object for which the society originally was founded in 1937. Maintained as a historic house museum, its neighborhood context now became a concern. There were, moreover, several other houses of significance in the Third Ward, and many of a historic character that seemed to warrant preservation. Some older residents still found the neighborhood a good place to live, and it was thought that many younger people in the community might be attracted by an improved neighborhood, convenient to the city center.

The impending large-scale destruction of the historic neighborhood was a crisis in the history of the Landmark Society. Not without some dissent, the organization began to shift the focus of its concern from individual historic buildings to broader problems of area preservation, environmental quality, and neighborhood vitality. Despite the advice of some who considered the problem too large, the time too late, and the organization too inexperienced, a major campaign was planned to try to save the Third Ward.

Most probably the success of the society in this and subsequent undertakings, such as the East Avenue Plan, derives largely from a cooperative attitude, although constructive criticism is sometimes required. It was apparent that redevelopment plans for the Third Ward could destroy most of the historic character, and the society worked with the Urban Renewal Agency; its recommendations were written into the urban renewal plan.

Realistically, initiative was needed to begin neighborhood improvement. Belief that the Third Ward could be a good place to live had to be based on more than plans and rhetoric. Attractive homes were needed to bring people to the neighborhood. Consequently, a corporation was sponsored by the society (deriving its capital from members of the society) to acquire and improve properties in the Third Ward. A revolving fund was used to buy and hold properties until owners could be found to rehabilitate them. At the time of transfer, restrictive covenants were placed on the deed to assure future preservation. This limited amount of risk capital proved to be sufficient, not as the sole means to reclaim this large area, but as evidence to others that investment was being made here, and thus to encourage confidence. Several members of the society as individuals acquired and improved properties, sometimes for their own use and sometimes as a challenging way of making a contribution.

140

Importantly, it has not been intended that the Third Ward become another Georgetown, or be reconstituted like some other well-known examples of residential neighborhood reclamation, which have succeeded in evicting original occupants in order to accommodate more affluent residents. Instead, the level of restoration has been appropriate for an attractive neighborhood, which is not a museum village.

Progress in the Third Ward was not dramatic at first. The patience and confidence of several years were required to realize appreciable change. Today, however, the area has been substantially reclaimed; virtually all of the historic properties available for rehabilitation have been acquired for this purpose. Certainly many individual properties await completion of improvements, but the success of the Third Ward campaign seems assured.

Approaching the Third Ward from downtown, the boundary of the area that was the Erie Canal has now become Broad Street. Built as a landmark next to the canal, Jonathan Child's grand house was constructed in 1837 at 37 South Washington Street (Plate 70). It has been said that the designer

70. Jonathan Child House, 37 South Washington Street, Rochester. Standing prominently near what used to be the Erie Canal, the Greek Revival mansion, built from the proceeds of canal trade by Rochester's first mayor, announces the Third Ward. It is a sumptuous example of the style, both outside and inside. There are five notable Corinthian columns on the portico, with one being in the center, where a space is usually anticipated. This is aligned with an interior partition dividing two parlors, so that the spaces between the columns correspond to the pairs of windows in the parlors. The entablature and pediment, with rich Greek ornament, as well as the window lintels, are finely detailed. The Child House, together with the neighboring Brewster-Burke House, is part of an important grouping.

was S. P. Hastings, although this is not known to be documented. Hastings is thought to have been responsible for at least two important houses in the Third Ward: the Jonathan Child House and the Hervey Ely House, discussed later in this chapter. The quality of the work here is evident on the exterior as well as the interior, where a beautiful spiral staircase descends into a light and spacious center hallway, extending the full width of the house, between side entrances with matching porticos. A crystal chandelier hangs from a handsome ceiling escutcheon, and the prominent woodwork is well detailed in the Greek Revival style. On the front of the house are twin parlors, divided by large sliding doors. Their windows open onto the main portico, with panels below the large double-hung sash, which may be opened to create doorways to the porch. The plaster ceilings are exceptionally rich, as are the massive black marble fireplaces and crystal chandeliers in these parlors. They convey an opulence worthy of a merchant prince and civic leader of the early nineteenth century. The dining room is on the other side of the hall, behind the staircase, with access from a small corridor. On the second floor, one bedroom retains a Greek Revival fireplace, to which unusual late-nineteenth-century tile has been added.

The Jonathan Child House was the third acquisition of the Landmark Society. After the Campbell-Whittlesey House in the Third Ward had been restored as a house museum, the society recognized that this building, which was in jeopardy, also warranted preservation. The property was purchased and leased in 1957 to the Bureau of Municipal Research (today the Center for Governmental Research). This proved to be a successful manner of adaptive use. Eventually the property was sold to the Research Corporation with restrictive covenants. Although used for offices, portions of the interior may be seen by the public, by prior arrangement with the Landmark Society.

The new users appreciated the value of the building and took considerable care to preserve and match original work when making necessary alterations. New partitions were designed so that they could be removed at a later date without causing any damage to original finishes. In time, the growth of the organization required additional space. The problem of adding new construction to a historic building was especially sensitive to the Landmark Society because it owned the neighboring building on the block, which it used for its headquarters. Because the Child House had been designated a landmark, the expansion proposal also afforded an initial exercise of responsibility for the newly ordained Rochester Preservation Board. The new board, rejecting the architect's first design proposal, proved itself to be no rubber stamp. A second design, as it now appears at the rear of the house, is lower and similar to the original work in some ways, without fraudulently claiming historic character.

Next to the Jonathan Child House, but fronting on Spring Street, at Number 130, is the remarkable building housing the administrative offices of the Landmark Society (Plate 71). Built in 1849 by Henry Brewster, it may have been designed by Henry Searle. Later, for a long period of time, it was the residence of the Burke family. In basic form, it is a center-entranced, two-floored house with bracketed eaves and a low pitched roof—features common to the Italianate style. But it is the exotic entrance porch that distinguishes the design most of all: a practically free-standing pavilion, appearing vaguely Moorish or Oriental. The ogee architectural motif is repeated on the lintels and the facade of the frame wing to the left of the house. The ornateness of the eaves brackets is consistent; fine iron balconies complete the effect. Investigation has shown that the house, inside and out, was originally painted with subtle gradations of the same cream-to-ocher range, including brick work, which has been restored.

The reaction to a quarter-century of neoclassicism is well expressed; in fact, the forms probably do not imitate specific models, but more likely are playful inventions. The unusual porch is not altogether unique; similar columns may be found on a simpler, slightly later porch in the neighborhood, that of the Hayden House, which will be seen later at 144 South Fitzhugh

Street. Possibly both may be the work of the same architect, or the latter example may have been influenced by the former. The 1849 Brewster-Burke House is a relatively early example of the Italianate, as compared to the 1856 Bates-Ryder House on East Avenue (Plate 29) and others. More typically, the Italianate period in Rochester occurred during the late 1850s and early 1860s. Greek Revival designs were still being built when this house was constructed. Its novelty, surprising today, must have astonished the Rochester of 1849.

The Landmark Society is adapting the interior of the Brewster-Burke House for exhibition, meeting, and office use. The John F. Wenrich Memorial Library of Local Architecture and Urban Planning has been established here. Considerable volunteer labor of members has contributed to the restoration of such features as false wood-grained woodwork on the interior. The painted glass entrance doors should also be noted. Before leaving, one may obtain a more detailed guide to a walking tour of the Third Ward, prepared by the Landmark Society and available at the Brewster-Burke House.

The front porch of the Brewster-Burke House now faces a major arterial highway that has cut through the old Third Ward, separating the greater portion on the far side from the downtown area. A pedestrian bridge, how-

71. **Brewster-Burke House,** 130 Spring Street, Rochester. Effective counterpoint to the Greek Revival house next door is provided by this exotic fantasy. Built in 1849, it evidences a new taste at the mid-century for novel forms, suggesting faraway places. The Brewster-Burke House is the headquarters of the Landmark Society.

ever, crosses the highway at this point. The demolition, so disruptive, has opened many of the landmarks to a more distant view. Before, this had been a tightly contained neighborhood. On the near side of the highway, to the left, across South Washington Street, is the 1910 Bevier Memorial Building, designed by Claude Bragdon and built as a facility of the Rochester Institute of Technology, which occupied many buildings in the Third Ward prior to construction of its new campus, to be seen later. On a corner of the Bevier Building is a plaque commemorating Nathaniel Rochester, who had built his home on the site.

In the adjoining block is the handsome First Presbyterian Church, with a prominent spire. Designed by A. J. Warner and built in 1871, the church at the corner of Plymouth Avenue and Spring Street houses the oldest religious congregation in the city. There are Tiffany glass windows and interior paneling and pews of black walnut.

Across the pedestrian bridge is an imposing Greek Revival house with columned portico. Built in 1837, about the same time as the nearby Jonathan Child House (Plate 70), the Hervey Ely House (Plate 72) also has been attributed to S. P. Hastings. Certainly a sure hand is evident, exhibiting the

72. **Hervey Ely House,** 138 Troup Street, Rochester. Doric columns and entablature here are in contrast to the Corinthian order of the Child House (Plate 70). Somewhat smaller in size than the Child House, this residence is no less monumental. The more sober dignity of the most chaste classical order prevails. Side wings of the period less correctly correspond to the original temple model, but the result is a pyramidal massing effectively adapted to the rising site. The house is owned and maintained by the Irondequoit Chapter of the Daughters of the American Revolution as its headquarters. The excellent interiors are of Greek Revival style.

Doric mode, as identified by the entablature and columns. There is good classical detail on the interior as well. The formal composition here contrasts with the Child House, which was planned with side entrances and a simple rectangular temple form. Here the entrance is located asymmetrically, with matching wings on either side.

The Child and Ely houses are built of masonry covered with painted stucco—a more substantial and finished manner of building than is the frame construction of the typical rural village or farmhouse, so characteristic of the Greek Revival. Both of these urbane buildings utilize a color to set off the white architectural features, whereas more familiar rural examples were painted entirely white. The interiors of these city houses of the period also used subtle gradations of color, pointing up decorative moldings and details. The Brewster-Burke House, it will be recalled, although about a decade later in date and style, is of painted brick. It is a popular misconception that the restoration of brick buildings should begin with cleaning paint from the masonry. Because soft, common brick was often used, paint was necessary to provide protection from the weather. Sandblasting may badly erode this material, as evidenced by some buildings in the neighborhood. Furthermore, the color of the building was often basic to the conception; in the instance of the Brewster-Burke House, exteriors and interiors were painted in a closely keyed color range.

A walk about a few typical blocks in the heart of the Third Ward is suggested by the map. Without knowing the condition of this area prior to rehabilitation, it may be difficult to appreciate the amazing transformation that has occurred (Plate 73). Not only have houses been reclaimed from impending demolition and attractively renovated, but streets, sidewalks, and curbs have been replaced, and new trees planted. It may be difficult to realize now the foresight required to initiate such an ambitious program in a neighborhood so far deteriorated, and to fully appreciate the courage of the first individuals who moved back into the neighborhood.

73. Greenwood Street, Rochester. These gabled frame houses, now restored and well maintained, evidence the success of the rehabilitation program encouraged by the Landmark Society.

150

One of the first buildings to be reclaimed in the area, and one of the first to serve as an example of the return of interest and concern on the part of residents of more secure districts and suburbs, is the charming little brick residence at 42 Atkinson Street. The architect Isaac Loomis built this house about 1850 for his own use.

The small, white frame cottage next door served as an interim headquarters of the Landmark Society when the Third Ward was one of its principal projects. The location of this cottage, in the midst of the daily life of the neighborhood, contributed valuably to successful community relations. Such communication has been missed somewhat since the headquarters has been relocated in larger facilities at the edge of the Third Ward, separated from the residential area by the arterial highway.

The two brick buildings flanking the entrance to Atkinson Street from Plymouth Avenue were built in the 1840s (Plate 74). The Amon Bronson House, built about 1844, is remarkable for the pair of two-story bow windows. Although the original wood-paneled Greek Revival door has been replaced by a later glass model, this distinguished building has otherwise been little al-

74. **Amon Bronson House** and **William Churchill House,** 263 and 249 South Plymouth Avenue, Rochester. The Bronson House is one of the most distinctive in the Third Ward and in the region; few Greek Revival designs incorporated curved features such as these bow windows, which seem to recall Boston. The Churchill House, across Atkinson Street, remained in the same family for generations, and despite changes in the neighborhood, it has been little altered since it was built in 1848.

tered. The classical columns of the porches on the Churchill House seem to be Greek Revival in character, but the low pitched roof with broad eaves suggests the emerging Italianate. It was constructed in 1848, four years after the Bronson House across the street, and one year before the Brewster-Burke House (Plate 71), which is similar in some ways, but different in its exotic character. Like the Bronson House, the Churchill House has been little altered.

Subsequent decades of the nineteenth century are well represented by other buildings on Plymouth Avenue, comprising an important collection. At this juncture, one may continue around the block directly to the Campbell-Whittlesey House, as shown on the map, or take a more extended circuit, also shown. Although the latter route presently reveals much of the demolition of the Third Ward resulting from urban renewal, it does pass Adams Street, now well maintained, and takes in the grouping around Plymouth Park at Edinburgh Street. The Colonel Henry Cady House of 1839 is the prominent anchor on a corner here, and has been returned to its historic character. Colonel Cady was the engineer for the second aqueduct, for which Charles F. Bissell, whose house was seen on East Avenue, was the principal contractor. The 1900 Corn Hill A.M.E. Zion Church, behind the Cady House, is a commendable example of conservation. After the church was gutted by fire, the congregation decided to rebuild the structure, retaining the tower and the entrance arch, which serves as a gateway to a new forecourt.

Plymouth Circle forms a focal point of the old Third Ward on Plymouth Avenue, its most important thoroughfare. Complementing the Corn Hill Church is the Roman Catholic Church of the Immaculate Conception, a brick Italianate building of 1864–73. Also, brick row houses, built about 1880, may be noted adjacent to the circle, at 47–57 Glasgow Street. Spared demolition by urban renewal, it is a type of housing not common here.

It has been proposed that a new school be built on nearby land, which has been cleared; no doubt, this will contribute importantly to the neighborhood. A particular loss has been a number of genuine local neighborhood in-

75. South Fitzhugh Street, Rochester. This attractive row of masonry, Italianate houses, with low hipped roofs and broad eaves, may be contrasted to the more modest frame houses on Greenwood Street.

stitutions, but as redevelopment continues, the whole range of community services and functions probably will be revived in the old Third Ward.

A loop back may be made by way of Fitzhugh Street (Plate 75). The notable porch of the Brewster-Burke House is recalled by the columns on a somewhat simpler porch at Number 144, the Charles J. Hayden House. Among other buildings warranting notice is the house at Number 138, built in 1852 (Plate 76). It is typical of many smaller houses of the time in the neighborhood, but it is enhanced by the special quality of the ironwork.

The Campbell-Whittlesey House (Plates 77–79), at the head of Fitzhugh Street, is of special significance in the community. Not only is it highly visible, with an imposing Ionic portico fronting on a modern arterial highway, but for decades it has served a unique educational and cultural role. During the Depression, this important old house was threatened, and the Landmark Society of Western New York was organized to acquire it and thus to preserve it. In more recent decades, community interest in the house has provided volunteers for a continuing educational program at the property. Numerous busloads of schoolchildren, in addition to many other visitors, visit the house annually. The building and its contents are excellently interpreted

76. **138 South Fitzhugh Street,** Rochester. Fine ironwork distinguishes this smaller house, built just before the Civil War. It has been adapted for use as offices without detracting from the residential quality of the neighborhood.

by members of the society and staff who serve as guides. A reconstructed herb garden is maintained by a garden club. Frequent changes of interior floral decorations and arrangements of artifacts reward the returning visitor.

On the exterior, the use of brick, without either stucco or paint, may be noted in contrast to the other mansions of similar style seen previously in the Third Ward. Although the entrances themselves are fairly simple in the usual manner, the detail of the Ionic portico is very fine, and the unusual console bracket and fretwork grills in the frieze band of the cornice should be noted. The fence, although a reconstruction, is in character; most yards at this time were similarly bounded.

The arrangement of the interior is similar to that of the Jonathan Child House, with a side entrance, and double parlors across the front, opening on to the portico. More modest, however, the hallway does not run through the house to a matching entrance on the other side, but is terminated by a small room, opening under the spiral stairway. A spacious dining room also opens from the hallway, to the left under the stairway. Behind this is a service corridor, with its own separate entrance on the street, off from which open a small office and the kitchen, with pantry and closets between. The cooking

77. Campbell-Whittlesey House, 123 South Fitzhugh Street, Rochester. One of the major landmarks of the county and the region, this is another of the important Greek Revival mansions of the Third Ward. The classical order employed here is Ionic. Characterized by grace, it is simpler than the rich Corinthian (Plate 70) and more elegant than the massive Doric (Plate 72). Even more interesting than

the fine classical portico at one end is the inventive form at the other—a non-symmetrical composition with a void beneath the heavy cornice, which is supported visually at the corner by a large, carved console bracket. The first acquisition of the Landmark Society, this 1835 house has been excellently restored and is open to the public.

fireplace in the kitchen is a reconstruction; elements elsewhere in the house are of unquestioned authenticity. The finishes, of course, have been changed many times in the long history of the house, but careful investigation revealed much of the original work, which has been largely reproduced. The unusual wallpaper in the dining room is not original, but is reproduced from old French blocks of unique design, incorporating Indian heads in the band at the top. The detail of the spiral stairway is good, and the curious arrangement beneath, where the cornice of the door frame dies in an irregular manner into a curved surface, is unique (Plate 78). The parlors are the principal rooms of the house (Plate 79). Although smaller than the Jonathan Child House, the Campbell-Whittlesey House has the same sense of gracious amplitude. The refinement of the architectural detail here and the subtlety of colors, in particular, yield a character somewhat less heavily grand.

The architect of this important building is not known; comparisons to the influential designs of Minard LaFever have been made (and a fine publication on the subject of the house is available there). LaFever's *The Modern Builder's Guide* was one of several pattern books of the early nineteenth century that were often used in the region as sources of models, especially for

78. Campbell-Whittlesey House, 123 South Fitzhugh Street, Rochester. Although little reconstruction was required for restoration of the interiors, duplication of original surfaces necessitated considerable research. The color combinations, elaborate but subtle, are a good example of successful reproduction. A publication available here describes the process of restoration.

architectural details such as the cased opening between the double parlors. Although LaFever produced designs for some important Greek Revival buildings in upstate New York, there is no documentation to warrant attribution of this house to him.

Built in 1835, the Campbell-Whittlesey House preceded by two years the Jonathan Child House and the Hervey Ely House. The Greek Revival mansions of East Avenue, it may be recalled, followed these Third Ward examples by a few years. Elsewhere in the county, buildings of the Federal style, such as those seen in Pittsford, were still being built in the 1830s and 1840s. The Campbell-Whittlesey House is one of the first significant Greek Revival buildings in Monroe County, initiating the new style that was to last almost fifteen years.

79. Campbell-Whittlesey House, 123 South Fitzhugh Street, Rochester. Furnishings and interior finishes were carefully selected to re-create early-nineteenth-century conditions. The intent was not to re-create a model Greek Revival interior, but to re-create a more typical room of the time, with a collection of pieces handed down in a family.

161

162

Concluding the circuit of the Third Ward, and returning to the bridge across the arterial highway, one passes the imposing mansions of Emmet Hollister and Charles E. Hart on Plymouth Avenue (Plate 80). Dating from 1864 and 1865, respectively, they evidence the finest taste of their decade, just as the Campbell-Whittlesey House represented the best of its own. The Italianate, by this date, had matured some fifteen years since the Brewster-Burke House appeared. The Second Empire style, with its characteristic mansard roof, must have appeared more up-to-date when these houses were constructed at the end of the Civil War. The new Powers Building (Plate 58) soon was to be built in the same French style; Anderson Hall (Plate 45) at the University of Rochester had appeared in this new mode several years earlier, in 1861. The 1860s seem to have been the decade of the mansard roof.

The prominence of the Hollister and Hart houses, which are now divided into apartments, warrants their being cherished among the most important landmarks of the Third Ward and the larger community.

80. Emmet Hollister House and **Charles E. Hart House,** 207–211 and 199 South Plymouth Avenue, Rochester. Equaling the visual importance of other major landmarks in the Third Ward, this pair of mansions serves as a familiar symbol of the neighborhood. Built only one year apart, they represent two concurrent, fashionable modes of the Civil War decade—the Italianate, and the Second Empire variations, both on a vertical theme.

8

MOUNT HOPE

Like the East Avenue and Third Ward areas, previously seen, Mount Hope long has been one of the city's finest residential areas. Situated south of the downtown like the Third Ward, but on the other side of the Genesee River, its character is somewhat different. The Third Ward is an older, more compact subdivision of small blocks, with houses generally tightly spaced. East Avenue is a more extended linear development of imposing structures, usually sited on generous plots, giving access to side streets with smaller houses of different character. Mount Hope Avenue, paralleling the river, likewise gives access to side streets containing good residential neighborhoods, but it is distinguished primarily by several important buildings erected on the acreage of the Ellwanger and Barry nurseries, and by verdant park and cemetery lands. The city has now designated this area the Mount Hope–Highland Preservation District.

The Mount Hope district is joined to the Third Ward by the Clarissa Street bridge across the Genesee River. Proceeding south, on the left-hand side of the avenue one sees an attractive group of houses, Numbers 548–566 (Plate 81), similar to each other in basic design but with considerable variety of detail. These were built by the firm of Ellwanger and Barry; the important commercial nurseries of this partnership were located farther up the hill.

81. Mount Hope Avenue, Numbers 548–566, Rochester. The Mount Hope district is characterized by many blocks of good residences, together with some distinguished mansions and splendid landscape. This row of houses is charming for its variety within a prevailing unity of form and scale. The buildings were well built of masonry, with stone trim and slate roofs and some fine detail in wood. The house second from the left, in particular, shows angular, stick-like adornments characteristic of the Eastlake style in the 1870s (Plate 6).

165

Shortly, one passes two larger residences somewhat screened by shrubbery on the right-hand side of the street. The first, Number 609, is a brick residence built by Henry Ellwanger; its style is similar to that of the smaller block of row houses previously seen and shows an Eastlake character of the 1870s in its lively angularity and elaborate wood detail. Next door, at Number 625, hardly visible from the avenue, is an older house originally built in 1839 by James Hawks, and enlarged and remodeled as an Ellwanger residence about the turn of the century. Most notable are the beautiful gardens (Plate 82), maintained by a granddaughter of one of the original nursery proprietors. Although that business was terminated long ago, the magnificent trees and spacious landscape of much of the Mount Hope area derive from this origin.

82. Ellwanger Gardens, 625 Mount Hope Avenue, Rochester. One of the finest in the county, this extensive garden continues the horticultural tradition established by a grandparent-founder of an important commercial nursery on Mount Hope.

The offices of the Ellwanger and Barry Nursery (Plates 3 and 83) were housed across the street, in a building designed in the Gothic Revival style by the nationally known architect Alexander Jackson Davis. Built in 1854, this work, excluding churches, is the major example of its style in the region and one of Mount Hope's historic landmarks.

83. **Ellwanger and Barry Nursery Office** and **Patrick Barry House,** 668 and 692 Mount Hope Avenue, Rochester. One of the most beautiful compositions of buildings and landscape in the region is attributable to the nurserymen who established the setting over a century ago, and to their taste in architects: Alexander Jackson Davis and Gervase Wheeler, respectively. The romantic setting is appropriate to the character of the buildings, which served as the nursery office and as the residence of one of the partners in the business. The office, built in 1854, has been illustrated as an example of Gothic Revival style (Plate 3). The house, begun the next year and completed in 1857, is an important example of the Italianate style. The unusual detail of the broad eaves is notable, as is the detail on the exterior and throughout the interiors.

The Patrick Barry House, another important structure in this complex, is one of the most splendid houses in Monroe County (Plates 83–86). Begun the year following construction of the offices, it was built between 1855 and 1857 from plans by Gervase Wheeler, nationally prominent for his published designs. Certainly this house compares with the Bates-Ryder House (Plate 29) of the same time as an outstanding example of the Italianate style.

84. Patrick Barry House and Carriage House, 692 Mount Hope Avenue, Rochester. A century-old landscape enhances this remarkable complex. The rounded and segmentally arched windows of the house reflect the new Italianate taste; the graceful tower is but one of many notable features of Gervase Wheeler's design.

Especially notable are the plaster ceilings of the interior, exquisitely detailed and painted in many colors. Throughout, the decor is sumptious, especially the rich window and door hangings. This is as splendid and significant an example of mid-nineteenth-century design and decorative art as the interiors of the Campbell-Whittlesey House (Plates 78 and 79) are of the earlier Greek Revival period, or the Oliver Culver Tavern (Plate 30) of the Federal style. Perhaps it is no coincidence that Miss Elizabeth Holahan has contributed her taste and expertise to all these interiors. As a work of restoration and period decoration, the Patrick Barry House is comparable to any in the region or elsewhere.

85. Patrick Barry House, 692 Mount Hope Avenue, Rochester. Finely detailed, superbly restored and furnished, these interiors are models of the mid-nineteenth century. The provost of the University of Rochester now lives here.

173

The verdant character of the district is continued by Mount Hope Cemetery and Highland Park, which were created from a portion of the Ellwanger and Barry Nursery property that had been given to the city. The cemetery, dedicated in 1838, displays a superb landscape composition (Plate 87). A picturesque stone Gothic Revival building, cast iron fountain, and wood gazebo (Plate 88), together with magnificent trees, are combined in one of the finest works of nineteenth-century art in the region. English landscape gardening, which attempts to transform a natural scene into an idealized state, is represented here.

86. Patrick Barry House, 692 Mount Hope Avenue, Rochester. Less sumptuous than the parlors, the dining room nevertheless grandly conveys the mid-nineteenth-century character. The detail of the plaster ceiling is superb, as is the richly painted ceiling cornice. A stenciled wainscot band combines with the marble fireplace, gilded mirror, and other furnishings of the period, such as the richly bordered carpet, to complete the splendid scene.

87. Mount Hope Cemetery, Mount Hope Avenue, Rochester. Like a romantic landscape painting, this picturesque composition embodies nineteenth-century idealized nature integrated with architecture, as so successfully accomplished at the nearby Ellwanger and Barry complex. The Gothic Revival chapel and cast iron fountain combine with a nearby gazebo in a setting dominated by magnificent trees.

88. Gazebo, Mount Hope Cemetery, Mount Hope Avenue, Rochester. Landmarks come in various sizes, such as this nineteenth-century folly.

177

Across Mount Hope Avenue from the cemetery is Warner Castle (Plate 89). It was built in 1854 from sketches made on writing paper by the owner, Horatio G. Warner, a bank president, court judge, and newspaper publisher. The amateur design probably should be regarded more as a folly than as a work comparable in merit to the nearby buildings designed by Davis and Wheeler, which were being built about the same time. Tradition indicates that an ancestral Scottish castle of the Clan Douglas was the intended association. Amusing as an untutored essay in medievalism as seen from upstate New York, it may be better to view the castle and its gatehouse as picturesque features in a larger landscape composition. Warner Castle, owned by the City of Rochester, has provided good adaptive use for the Rochester Garden Center.

Many attractive and comfortable residential streets were developed off Mount Hope Avenue, and together with the more prominent features of the district, they comprise a particularly green and serene quarter of the city. Highland Park, also across Mount Hope Avenue from the cemetery, is well known, particularly for the spectacular display at lilac time, which draws visitors from afar.

Between Mount Hope Cemetery and the Genesee River is the University of Rochester; beyond the campus, Genesee Valley Park extends the green character of this section of the city along the river. A visitor following a restricted itinerary might continue from this point to the Rochester Institute of Technology, Scottsville, and Mumford. A visitor with more leisure time is urged to make a broader circuit by way of the lake to Clarkson, a small village that is one of the historic treasures of the county.

89. Warner Castle, 5 Castle Park (off Mount Hope Avenue), Rochester. A curiosity, less significant for its architectural value than as part of a larger landscape composition, this stone, castellated structure expresses the mid-nineteenth-century taste for the remote in time and place.

9

SEVERAL COUNTY VILLAGES, THE R.I.T. CAMPUS, AND THE GENESEE COUNTRY MUSEUM

Monroe County, although dominated by metropolitan Rochester, is far from being wholly urbanized. Many farms and rural villages can still be found. A few representative town and rural structures have been selected to be visited; they may be seen by following a convenient circuit of limited extent and duration. The itinerary includes the new campus of the Rochester Institute of Technology (R.I.T.).

The visitor should allow at least a full day for the tour; with more than one day, the visitor could enjoy less hurried walks about the towns and the campus.

Clarkson, Brockport, Scottsville, Mumford, and Honeoye Falls are attractive and historic villages, each with its own character. Clarkson is still a crossroads town. It grew up on the lake plain where the Ridge Road was crossed by a north-south route leading to the lake. After the Erie Canal, now the Barge Canal, was constructed a few miles south of Clarkson, the neighboring village of Brockport grew up as a more important commercial center of the area. A true canal town, as the name suggests, it retains business blocks evidencing the prosperity of the nineteenth century. In the southwest corner of the county are Scottsville and Mumford. Scottsville is a white-painted Greek Revival village of tree-lined streets, in contrast to the older, brick Federal architecture of Clarkson and to the nineteenth-century commercial character of Brockport. Shortly beyond Scottsville is the rural hamlet of Mumford; nearby an important museum village has been reconstructed. Returning eastward, and completing a circuit around the county, one finds Honeoye Falls, with some handsome stone buildings pleasantly situated on a picturesque stream. On route between these villages is the R.I.T. campus, one of the major works of modern architecture in New York State.

Rochester was developed at the junction of the Erie Canal and the Genesee River, a short distance from Lake Ontario. The city has expanded to the lake, about six miles north of the downtown. The geographical context of the community can be more fully appreciated by driving to the western portion of the county by way of the lakeshore. Traveling northward from the Four Corners on State Street, which becomes Lake Avenue, one passes the offices and main works of the Eastman Kodak Company, on the route paralleling the Genesee River; one then crosses Ridge Road. This was a major historic route across the county, and it leads westward directly to Clarkson, the first village to be visited. The continuation of Lake Avenue northward leads to the Lake Ontario Parkway, a more scenic route to Clarkson, as indicated by the map.

The village green at Clarkson extends between Ridge Road and the Congregational church, marked by a white spire rising above the treetops. This is a good point of departure for a walk through this historic village (as suggested on the accompanying map). The Congregational church was built in 1825, following traditional New England models. The interiors were probably remodeled in 1869, when the church became Presbyterian (for a second time). The round-headed windows are Italianate in style, suggesting the Civil War era. It was about this time that stained glass became widespread in use, and most old churches were updated with new windows. The original buildings probably had large, double-hung sash with small panes and clear glass. Otherwise the church has not been much altered on the exterior. It retains original pilasters, entablature, and pediment, framing a distinctive fan in the Federal style. The tower appears to be original, except for its spire, which seems to have been replaced or added in the later nineteenth century.

182

Next to the church on the green is the old Clarkson Academy (Plate 90), which replaced an older structure that had burned. The brick building of 1853 is a good example of a pre–Civil War schoolhouse. It might become a community center or a bank, or serve any number of adaptive uses, particularly if the village should grow. Worth saving, it is part of an important grouping on the village green, in the center of a richly historic village.

90. Clarkson Academy, 8343 Ridge Road West, Clarkson. The pre–Civil War schoolhouse on the green in Clarkson complements a white, spired church from the Federal period, contributing to a valuable grouping. The Greek Revival character prevails, and the brick is from a brickyard that existed here since the early nineteenth century. Now unused, the old academy building presents a preservation problem, since the community is so small. It nevertheless has good potential for adaptive use and should be maintained as a centerpiece in this historic collection.

Many of the houses on Ridge Road are quite old, one being marked as the 1820 birthplace of the astronomer Lewis Swift. Some of these have been altered to varying degrees, although original features often may be discerned. Virtually unchanged, however, is the Albert Palmer House (Plate 91), one of the most important Federal buildings of the region. Built in the early 1820s, the entrance is unusually elaborate: above an original paneled door is a splendid fanlight, with delicate metal work radiating from an eagle. The cornice of the doorway, broken in plan, is a feature of the style frequently used on mantlepieces, but less commonly employed in the manner seen here, supported on curved and fluted brackets. The same fine fluting appears on the small pilasters around door and side lights. Although there is not as much carving in-the-round on this entrance as appears on some Clarkson doorways, the overall design is unusual. As a whole, the house is of special value as an example of Federal design.

91. **Albert Palmer House,** 8251 Ridge Road West, Clarkson. One of the best in this village or hereabouts, this excellent example of Federal design was built in the 1820s. Although doorways with elliptical fanlights and side lights of varied design are a characteristic feature of Clarkson (Plates 92 and 1, 93), this early example is distinctive for the elaborate frame surrounding the entrance. Flush boarding was used on the front, and beveled siding elsewhere—a practice of the time. The elegant detail of the pedimented gable, framing an elliptical fan, together with the attenuated pilasters at the corner (with unusual capitals), express the taste of the Federal period.

Returning past the village green to the main intersection, turning onto Lake Road, one finds the richest collection of historic buildings in the village, and one of the best in the county. For some reason, this row of fine houses was built on one side of the street only, the west side. More modern construction now is found on the east side, although an old cobblestone shop (now, unfortunately, with a stucco front) is situated there. A walk may be taken up the newer side to view the row of important houses from across the street, then return on the other side to see them at closer range. Six brick houses in a row vary in nineteenth-century style, as they were built over a thirty-year period.

At the far end is the Judge John Bowman House at Number 3797, built in 1824 (Plate 92). Part of a working farm, this building has not been treated as kindly through the years as the others; unfortunately, a picture window has been added in recent times. Nevertheless, the entrance here is a good one, of a type seen in many variations throughout the village.

92. **Judge John Bowman House,** 3797 Lake Road, Clarkson. This fine doorway, despite its neglect, is a good example of Federal practice in Clarkson. Showing elliptical fanlight and side lights between engaged colonnettes, the designs of these entrances vary subtly, particularly in the glazing pattern of the transom and side lights. The grace of the Federal style is evident in the delicately modeled Ionic colonnettes; although characteristically elongated, they have received careful entasis (the subtle curvature, of Greek origin, that makes them other than simple cylinders). The door here appears to be original. The elliptical lintel and the sill are of cut stone.

Next is the Simeon B. Jewett House at Number 3779 (Plates 1 and 93), built four years later, in 1828. This house is an excellent example of the Federal style, and its setting is appropriate and attractive.

A third brick house of the 1820s follows, the Henry Martyn House at Number 3773. Although the bracketed eaves and large paned sash probably date from the post–Civil War era, and although the porch across the front (despite its Greek Revival character) may be more modern, the original Federal entrance is splendid, and the design of its fan- and side-light patterns is distinctive.

Next door is the Lemuel Haskell House, built about twelve years later, in 1841. The simple porch suggests the later Greek Revival, but curiously the columns do not match, suggesting that the work actually may have been reconstructed at a later date from earlier pieces. The main entrance door is of the Greek Revival style, as are the doors of the side porch. The porch itself, however, is Italianate and is a handsome example of this later mode.

93. **Simeon B. Jewett House,** 3779 Lake Road, Clarkson. Just as the Palmer House (Plate 91) is one of the best regional examples of a Federal frame house, the Jewett House is one of the best Federal brick houses to be found in the area. It was built only a few years after the Palmer House (both in the 1820s) and again shows the characteristic Federal entrance common to both houses and to many others in the village. This one is very fine; it is illustrated more closely in Plate 1, representing the style. The decorative metal rain leader boxes, under the eaves of the roof at the corners, also are distinctive examples of their kind. The windows are generous in size, but a consistent small scale is maintained by the twelve-over-twelve sash with delicate muntins. The setting is appropriate as well as attractive, with the brick walk and fence, so typical of these houses when they were built.

The David Lee House, at Number 3749 (Plate 94), was built in 1840, about the same time as the Haskell House but is a purer example of the Greek Revival. It provides an interesting comparison with the Federal-style Jewett House (Plates 1 and 93), being similar in basic form, with three windows across the second floor and two below, with an entrance to one side. Here a wing has been added, and the gable turned towards the street (a preferred arrangement of the later period). The increased scale is apparent throughout: the more massive entrance, for example, and the six-over-six sash. Although the windows actually are smaller in size, they have received larger panes, more appropriate in scale. Larger pieces of glass were becoming available around 1840, and this size pane probably represents the maximum in common use here at the time.

The three principal architectural monuments of Clarkson are the Palmer and Jewett houses, which are frame and brick representatives of the Federal style, and the building next seen, the John Bowman House at Number

94. **David Lee House,** 3749 Lake Road, Clarkson. With gable end facing the street and a side wing balancing the off-center doorway, this 1840 house is one of the familiar Greek Revival types. Although detail may be less delicate than that of the Federal style, with simpler transom and side lights at the entrance, the design of the paneled door and surrounding frame evidences care. The columns of the side porch, with their incised design, and the circular window in the pediment, with its white frame offset to expose a band of brick, show the same attention to detail. Lintels are flat arches of brick; throughout, the masonry shows beaded mortar joints.

192

3741, a splendid example of the Greek Revival style (Plate 95). Built in 1850, its relatively late date is suggested by the richness and complexity of form and the detailed development. It is less true to the archaic temple models than are the three important examples seen in the Third Ward, even with wings added to a basic rectangular form, as seen on the Ely House (Plate 72). The basic composition here seems more baroque than Greek. The use of different scales on the same building is an adaptation, as is the concept of a glazed cupola.

In form this Greek Revival example is more akin to the group of three mansions seen on East Avenue, which were essentially square boxes with center entrances. The Woodside cupola (Plate 40) may be recalled as a precedent for this feature a decade earlier. To the large blocks of all of the East Avenue examples, smaller porticos were attached, as seen here. Those porches, however, were smaller in scale than these, being only one story high; and none received pediments such as are seen on these porches. Although the wedding of the pitched-roofed porticos to the main block of the mansion may not be regarded as adroit a solution as those seen either in the Third Ward or on East Avenue, the grandeur of the John Bowman House is unmistakable.

95. John Bowman House, 3741 Lake Road, Clarkson. In the late flowering of the Greek Revival, this house of 1850 follows by some fifteen years the earlier models seen in the Third Ward. Like the later examples of East Avenue, it is more square than rectangular, with the porticos affixed to the major and minor elevations. The central plan is expressed by a surmounting cupola, with pediments on all sides, defining the center in a pyramidal composition. Detail is good, with notable columns of the main portico repeated beside the main entrance. The unusual composition incorporates three central windows of the second floor between two large pilasters. The portico of the side entrance is of a contrasting Doric order.

194

This splendor never was enjoyed by those for whom it was built. According to local tradition, it was constructed for an intended bride. Before the wedding, however, the future master of the house departed suddenly, without explanation, for New York, and never returned. For the rest of her life, it is said, the jilted lady (who never married) dressed in mourning and avoided looking at the house that was to have been her home.

The property in more recent times has become a very comfortable residence. It is well built and well maintained; window lintels and sills are of cut stone, and the basement is stuccoed, with painted mortar joints. Surrounded by pleasant grounds, the house remains one of the important landmarks of village and county.

Continuing south about a mile on Lake Road, the visitor reaches the neighboring village of Brockport. Beyond the bridge crossing the canal is the business district (Plate 96), which retains many elaborate commercial buildings of the later nineteenth century. Like many a "Main Street, USA," the sidewalk level has been modernized and cannot be regarded as being more attractive now than it was a century ago. Nevertheless, the upper portions of the buildings form an ensemble that expresses the proud prosperity of its time.

96. Commercial Buildings, 1 Main Street, 9 and 13 Market Street, Brockport. The prosperity of this Erie Canal village during the mid-nineteenth century is evidenced by a good collection of brick and cast iron commercial buildings. Supposed improvement through modernization has destroyed the originally unified character of many such townscapes, but some small rural villages still retain fine examples of richly decorative work, particularly on the upper stories of their commercial buildings. Before such historic character is replaced by standardized shopping centers, commercial districts of villages such as Brockport should be assured of preservation.

Shortly beyond the shopping district, at 151 Main Street, is the Morgan-Manning House (Plate 97). Built in 1854, the new mid-century fashion for the Italianate is apparent. The square block of the basic house, with its center entrance, is not so different in kind from earlier models, but it wears a different dress. This example, perhaps, is not as appropriately termed an "Italian villa" as are some examples of the style, such as the Bates-Ryder House on East Avenue (Plate 29), which is more irregular in shape, with a square tower. But here again, low hipped roofs and broad eaves are seen, and the extended porch is a recurring feature of the Italianate style. The columns here are unusually massive. Tall, richly paneled, double entrance doors are another feature common to the later nineteenth century, like richly ornamented window lintels. Muntins subdividing sash into smaller scaled units disappeared as large panes of glass became available. The transformation at mid-century of the basic square house is remarkable.

In recent years the Morgan-Manning House was willed to public use without specification of a recipient. The Landmark Society was awarded the property and supervised its restoration by the newly formed Western Monroe Historical Society for use as a community center. It has since been deeded permanently to the Historical Society, with restrictive covenants to ensure its preservation. It is a credit to many people that this important and handsome house has been so well restored in a relatively short time.

97. **Morgan-Manning House,** 151 Main Street, Brockport. Morgan's Italianate mansion, constructed on Main Street in 1854, is another expression of the prosperity of this nineteenth-century village. The Greek Revival Bowman mansion in neighboring Clarkson (Plate 95) was built only four years before the Morgan-Manning House. The nineteenth-century front porch was a popular feature of the newer style. Stretching the full width of the house, more richly inventive columns

were raised atop pedestals, connected by a decorative railing. The classical entablature above the columns is replaced by broad eaves supported by brackets, one of the most familiar features of the Italianate mode. The Greek Revival cupola, as seen on earlier examples, has been converted by similar means into another familiar Italianate feature. Now the property of the Western Monroe Historical Society, the house is open to the public.

On the way to Scottsville and Mumford, in the southwest corner of the county, one may stop at the new campus of the Rochester Institute of Technology (Plate 98). One of the finest major works of the region in our own time is this entirely new, thirteen-hundred-acre campus complex, accommodating fourteen thousand students. Costing approximately sixty million dollars, it includes thirteen academic buildings and dormitories. A model of institutional planning, the complex is the result of collaboration between outstanding designers from across the country: Lawrence B. Anderson, the principal coordinating architect, together with Edward Larrabee Barnes, Kevin Roche and John Dinkeloo, Hugh Stubbins, Harry M. Weese, and the landscape architect Dan Kiley. Completed in 1968, the work evidences remarkable unity of conception and material expression, despite the individuality of the designers, whose personal styles may be recognized in the different buildings. Reproduced in publications around the world, the consistent but varied brick forms have been influential afar. Perhaps most significantly, the remarkable opportunity to design such a vast development comprehensively, has provided a model not only for other new institutions, but for new towns, suggesting that characteristic variety may be attained by several talented designers in their individual works, while overall harmony may prevail when there is agreement to work within a common design language.

98. Rochester Institute of Technology, 1 Lomb Memorial Drive, Henrietta. Widely influential on new architecture, this model is highly regarded as a collaborative design. Several well-known architects planned buildings employing brick in a contemporary idiom of the late 1960s. The building illustrated is the work of Kevin Roche and John Dinkeloo of Connecticut.

From the R.I.T. campus, the road to Scottsville, as shown on the map, follows the Genesee River. This was an old Indian trail; today it passes through extensive horse paddocks and pastures of the Wehle Estate. Although some new construction appears at the margins of Scottsville, the village has not grown appreciably or changed much during the last century. Scottsville is different from Clarkson: whereas the village on the lake plain is largely constructed of local brick, the town in the rolling southern meadowland is made up mostly of white-painted frame houses; while the earlier village is largely Federal, the later is Greek Revival in style.

A walking tour around several blocks of Scottsville is recommended, beginning at the small shopping area in the village center. There is less of the mid-nineteenth-century character of Brockport here, and many of the commercial buildings are older. On the south side of Main Street, towards the center of the block, is an old inn, a symmetrical Federal building of frame construction. Now an automatic laundry, the design repeats on the second story a slightly smaller version of the door and side lights on the ground level, recalling the arrangement of the Spring House (Plate 19). Possibly this opened originally onto a second-floor gallery. Two-over-two sash on the second floor have replaced smaller-paned windows, and the large openings on the ground floor are modern. Nevertheless, this is a rare survival of a frame public building from the early period of the county.

On the opposite side of the street, an interesting grouping of small commercial buildings combine brick, cobblestone, and wood. A recessed, two-story brick block, with a fine cast iron balcony, shows a corbeled cornice of a type common to brick buildings in the Greek Revival period. Another similar cornice may be noted on this street. The cobblestone structure next door reveals original stone pillars at the corners; at the entrance, decorative cast iron, square columns bear the maker's name of Cheney. Note as well the stone quoins at the corners and the coursing of cobbles on the side wall.

99. 10 Rochester Street, Scottsville. The Greek Revival in upstate New York arrived as a style at the time when the Erie Canal and new turnpikes were opening the region to more intensive settlement. Although many urban neighborhoods have changed considerably, the countryside is still characterized by a Greek Revival vernacular of white-painted houses. Their familiar simplicity and robustness seem to convey a regional character. This small-town house is symmetrical, except for the placement of the entrance. Detail is spare and simple, but heavily modeled cornices and moldings enrich the plain wooden boxes, casting shadows and varying scale. Large windows, like the metal fence, suggest the date c. 1850, when this portion of the house was built.

100. Edson House, 7 Rochester Street, Scottsville. Seeming almost to be an idealization of nineteenth-century upstate New York, this village scene, with a fine old house set amid trees, is especially nostalgic for its fence, as such fences were once an important part of the typical street scene. One of the common forms of

Rochester Street, as the name suggests, is the principal entry from that direction—the route by which the village was approached according to our itinerary. On entering, the visitor may have appreciated the general character, but closer observation on foot will better reveal many fine old houses, only a few of which may be pointed out here. A brick building at Number 8 is said to have been built about 1816. Large windows are notable for such early work. The entrance dates from 1927, when the interiors were largely remodeled.

The very good Greek Revival frame house at Number 10 (Plate 99) is associated with the architectural historian Carl Schmidt, who resided here for many years. The one-over-one sash on the second floor might have had smaller panes in an earlier version. The design of the fence suggests a later, Gothic Revival style, but as this is a later Greek Revival house, built about 1850, the total character is one of the mid-century. (A rear portion of the house, like many, is dated earlier—in this instance, about 1830.)

Across the street, behind another fence, is the larger Edson House (Plate 100), also associated for many years with the Skivington family. Like the house across the way, a portion of this building, said to have been built in 1816, must predate the more apparent Greek Revival work of 1846. Many old houses began as small cottages, which were later incorporated into an enlarged structure. The older portion here may be the side wing. The general appearance of the house, however, well represents the flowering of the Greek Revival style in the 1840s.

Greek Revival house was this sort of center-entranced block, with five windows across the second story, following a familiar plan that appears in preceding and subsequent styles. In this instance, large-scaled corner pilasters and entablature, with decorative iron grills set in the frieze band, typify the style.

The six-over-six windows of the Edson House are large; iron grills of the frieze band are related to a larger grill located in the pediment of the south gable. The handsome surroundings and splendid preservation of this fine house make it one of the outstanding examples of its kind in the county.

Just as the Federal style lingered locally, the Greek Revival also was persistent, especially in Scottsville—perhaps because of the influence of so many good examples at hand. Here, beyond the date when one expects to find them, Greek Revival elements appear on buildings that otherwise seem to be later in date. These and many other features of several periods may be observed on the suggested walk about the village.

Grace Episcopal Church is of a different period and character, but it is a valuable part of this collection of historic buildings (Plates 7 and 101). Built in 1885, its size and simplicity suggest a restricted budget; the firm of Charles and Harvey Ellis donated their professional services. It has been suggested that the model for the plan came from published sources (and the influence of pattern books and periodicals of the nineteenth century should not be underestimated), but the talented hand of Harvey Ellis seems to be evident.

101. Grace Episcopal Church, Browns Avenue, Scottsville. A modest church, creatively reinterpreting traditional forms and materials, attractively expresses the taste of the 1880s and of the talented Harvey Ellis. The Romanesque origins of the Richardsonian style, on the interior as well as the exterior (Plate 7), have become remote. Scale and character are domestic; warm, natural materials clearly express structure, with a minimum of superficial adornment.

205

On the exterior a rough cobblestone and field stone base rises to window sill height, above which there is a nonstructural curtain wall of stained glass and wood panels, some of these bearing the Yin and Yang device in wood relief. The roof is carried independently on interior columns, allowing the glazed enclosure, in contrast to the solidity of the stone base, to convey a curtainlike lightness. The entrance front is equally distinctive. Corbeled stone brackets carry a broad hood over both the doors and the stained glass windows located between them, extending the full width of the church. Shingles are employed in the gable, which frames a pointed arch filled with stained glass. This is surmounted by a projecting hood, semicircular in plan, carrying a cross.

The church is entered through an intimate vestibule, warmly lighted by the stained glass. Here, as in the interior, the simple and bold windows of the 1880s contribute the principal decorative quality. The floor of the nave slopes downward from the entrance; overhead the dark pattern of wood trusses is contrasted with the brilliance of curious crystal chandeliers, which may have been designed by the architect. At the sides, above dark pews and wood wainscoting, shines an almost continuous wall of luminous glass.

The plan is cruciform, with a suggestion of transepts and with a chancel arrangement typical of Episcopal churches. The furniture seems to be consistent with the pulpit and may have been designed by Ellis, although it does not match the pulpit. On the wall at either side of the chancel arch, plaster pilasters are topped with urns in relief, virtually the only decoration of the interior other than that which is afforded by the exposed wood structure and the colored glass. One may note that the 1945 window is inferior in decorative quality to the glass of sixty years earlier, simple though that may be. Fortunately, only one piece of the older glass has been replaced by more modern work.

Small and unassuming as it is, Grace Episcopal Church is a delight. It suggests not only the fresh talents of Harvey Ellis, but also the character of

102. Church Street, Scottsville. Increasingly valuable are neighborhoods of such quality and livability. The character of an area as a whole is worth more than the sum of its parts, even when they are historic buildings. The conservation of districts, with trees, fences, gardens, and serenity, is more important than preservation of single historic monuments.

those post–Civil War decades so often maligned in cultural criticism. As has been suggested, not only in the work of such masters as Richardson but also in the works of such lesser known figures as Ellis, as evidenced by this country church in upstate New York, there is an element of invention, taste, and joy not always so characteristic of design in subsequent periods.

Nearby is a brick, Italianate schoolhouse and a white frame church that also shows Italianate influence. The neighboring religious and academic structures recall the pair of buildings recently seen in Clarkson; the problem of finding reuse for the school is similar here as well. The church, like that in Clarkson, is of wood frame, with a basic meeting house form. An Italianate character is suggested by the round arches. The banding of the facade, breaking it into panels of clapboards, was a device of the mid-century, often found coupled with the sort of round window here appearing in the gable.

Shown together with the Union Presbyterian Church (Plate 102) is the John Dorr House, built about 1840 (Plate 103). A small residence, it is of a form found frequently in rural villages of New York State. The splendid doorway remains as a model of the style. Carl Schmidt, a resident of Scottsville, has recorded many such Greek Revival entrances among his studies of regional historic architecture.

103. John Dorr House, 17 Church Street, Scottsville. In each period, regardless of its stylistic language, exceptional examples eloquently express a generation of builders. This small frame house, on a side street in a rural village, shows a Greek Revival doorway that, in its own characteristic form, is as beautiful as any in the county.

Although more time might be spent in Scottsville, as elsewhere in the county, our itinerary moves on to nearby Mumford and the Genesee Country Museum. The countryside en route is pleasant, marked with historic buildings. One of the county's smallest landmarks is a little tailor's shop at a rural crossing. It is comparable in size to the "Little House," seen in Pittsford; both were early, diminutive commercial buildings. The style of the earlier lawyer's office, however, was Federal, and this is Greek Revival. The tailor who built this little shop is said to have operated the first sewing machine in Monroe County. His customers, however, scorned mechanical work so that he had to restrict it to hidden seams, finishing the visible sewing by hand. In later times the manufacture of clothing (particularly men's suits) was to become important to the regional economy.

Mumford today hardly is more than a crossroads marked by a few old buildings. The Exchange Hotel of 1835 (Plate 104) has recently been restored as the Mumford Community Building. It is a genuine landmark of this route, the sort of simple structure evidencing the taste of its time, which makes one wonder if modern buildings will prove to be as durably beautiful and useful.

104. **Exchange Hotel,** Main and George streets, Mumford. Another of several nineteenth-century inns scattered around the county, this simple building of 1835 has been restored to serve as a community center and headquarters for a fire district. It is similar in basic form to many of the old inns; the center entrance, repeated by a smaller side door, reflects a plan seen in the Federal examples at Pittsford (Plate 14) and the Oliver Culver Tavern off East Avenue (Plate 30). The simplicity of this country inn is refreshing and almost without style.

211

A short drive from this corner leads to the Genesee Country Museum in the southwest corner of the county (Plates 105–107). Now being prepared for opening to the public, the museum is a remarkable collection of early-nineteenth-century buildings reassembled here in an attractive arrangement simulating a village of the time. The general townscape is appealing, as are the individual structures and their interiors. Although every one of these buildings is authentic, few local towns were enriched with such a collection of superb designs. Time has stopped, with everything looking as though it were built just yesterday, prior to the Civil War. Federal and Greek Revival styles are mixed, as they would have naturally occurred in their original context.

One should not compare the Genesee Country Museum to real communities such as Pittsford, Clarkson, and Scottsville. Its purpose is otherwise —not a place in which to live, but a place to be educational and entertaining. The historical collection of architecture and artifacts assembled by the Genesee Country Museum comprises a magnificent gift to the history and culture of New York State.

Reconstruction and restoration have been carried on under the direction of Stuart Bolger, who made a knowledgeable contribution to the Landmark Society's restoration of the Stone-Tolan House on East Avenue (Plates 23 and 24). Considering the difficulties inherent in conveying a sense of oldness in newly restored buildings, as well as the problem of suggesting a commonplace context for an uncommon collection of superior objects, the exhibition here of early-nineteenth-century design and craft of the region has been splendidly conceived and executed.

Much as the first preference of preservation would be retention of structures in living use in their original situation, most of these beautiful buildings would have been destroyed without such a haven to receive them. One wishes that so many more valuable things from the past might have similarly been rescued.

105. Genesee Country Museum, Mumford. From various places in the region, important historic buildings, which otherwise might have been lost, have been brought to this museum village. Arranged around a village green is a valuable collection of beautifully restored Federal and Greek Revival structures. The collection continues to be augmented, as new structures are moved here and as interiors continue to be furnished.

The examples of log construction in the museum should not be misinterpreted. Log building was common throughout the nineteenth century, as long as timber was plentiful, and one should be cautious about a log-cabin myth which would suggest that this more primitive sort of construction preceded more finished work. In fact, many of the earliest houses of pioneer settlers were highly refined works of Federal architecture, while poorer and more utilitarian log cottages continued to be built for generations.

106. 1836 House, Genesee Country Museum, Mumford. Everything at the museum village warrants attention—which is its reason for being here—but we select only an example: a house of the late Federal style that was moved here from Pavilion, New York. The entrance arrangement is unusual; behind the door, which is surmounted by a window, there is a two-story-high space.

216

The Genesee Country Museum is expected to be open to the public in 1976. In time, the historical perspective of the museum may be expanded by the addition of mid-century and later buildings. Already it is a remarkable and worthwhile accomplishment, destined to be one of the principal features of the county.

107. **Hosmer Inn,** Genesee Country Museum, Mumford. The landlord's bedroom has been refurnished in the character of the early nineteenth century, with appropriate wallpaper and carpet as well as furniture and artifacts to suggest its everyday use.

The completion of the tour will bring the visitor to Honeoye Falls, a village directly south of Rochester. It is a mill town that grew on the banks of Honeoye Creek, which was dammed to create water power for its stone mills. There are two of these, the Upper Mill and the Lower Mill, built about 1827 and 1829, respectively. Both produced flour. The first to be seen, as suggested by the map, is the Lower Mill (Plate 108). Water from some distance upstream was carried through a sluice to operate the grinding equipment. Although unused and unrestored, this fine old structure is located near the attractive stream that connects it to the village center and the Upper Mill, which has become a pleasant restaurant. Perhaps similar adaptive use may be provided for the Lower Mill, related to the scenic and recreational resources of the stream and its wooded banks. In time a waterside walk may be possible.

108. **Lower Mill,** 61 North Main Street, Honeoye Falls. A fine old structure, this mill was built for utilitarian purposes. Historic character is conveyed by its stone walls. Located by a stream that flows through the center of the village, this now-vacant building has potential for good adaptive use as part of a larger scenic and recreational complex.

219

220

North Main Street leads to the village center, passing the Presbyterian church (Plate 109). This was erected in 1842, during that decade which seems to have been so productive of Greek Revival work in the county. Martin Pierce was the builder, and probably the designer as well. In those days professional practice was not so clearly established as it is today, and frequently builders were also designers, relying upon popular pattern books for assistance.

109. Presbyterian church, 27 North Main Street, Honeoye Falls. One of two landmark churches in the village, this is an example of the Greek Revival style. The wedding of a classical portico to the traditional meeting house form presented no great design problems, although the traditional spire, deriving from medieval precedent, was less easily rendered classical. Here it has been modeled of cubic elements, arranged pyramidally in a manner consistent in scale and detail to the building below. Not as refined as some urban works of the period, this is nevertheless a good representation of a Greek Revival rural church.

At the main intersection is the Wilcox House (Plate 110), a mid-nineteenth-century hotel that was enlarged from an earlier inn. The date of original construction is given as 1827, but most probably only that segment appearing as the lower two floors at the right-hand side of the building was constructed at that time. That portion is consistent with the practice observed in other country inns of the period. The second-floor doorway appears above a lower-floor entrance, as seen elsewhere, flanked by a pair of windows on each side on the second level. Probably before modernization two pairs of similar windows were located on either side of the ground floor entrance, comprising a symmetrical facade. The style of the enlarged building suggests the Greek Revival influence; the decorative enrichment of the cornice recalls similar brick details of the time seen elsewhere, even if not usually as elaborate as this. Located prominently at the main intersection, next to Honeoye Creek, this large historic building functions as a genuine landmark of the village.

110. **Wilcox House,** 3 North Main Street, Honeoye Falls. The last of several nineteenth-century inns to be seen on the tour, this somewhat larger hotel (now a Masonic Temple) characterizes the mid-nineteenth century, although a portion of it dates from an earlier period. The massive cornice suggests the Greek Revival and incorporates decorative brick work of the sort appearing before the Civil War. The six-over-six sash also remain from that era, although the ground floor, unfortunately, has been altered.

A few steps away, on West Main Street, is the Upper Mill (Plate 111). Like the church and the hotel at the crossroads, this is another important feature of the community, prominently situated near the town center, overlooking an attractive mill pond and stream. It is now a restaurant, effectively utilizing its historic character and scenic location.

Before going into the Upper Mill for a wayfarer-welcome, the visitor may wish to see the unusual stone Episcopal church on nearby Episcopal Avenue. Built in 1841–42, St. John's combines Greek and Gothic features, recalling the early Gothic Revival style introduced to the region by St. Luke's Episcopal Church of 1824 (Plates 67 and 69). Honeoye Falls will further reward the more curious visitor with fine buildings such as the stone Greek Revival House at 13 Maplewood Avenue and the Eastlake-style house at 37 Ontario Street (Plate 6).

The interest of the community in the quality of its surroundings is shown by other characteristics, such as the signs in the shopping area that conform to an overall plan. The development of the stream banks into a park is intended and soon may become another notable accomplishment of the village. Pleasant in any season, Honeoye Falls, with its Upper Mill, is an enjoyable place to end our tour of Monroe County.

111. Upper Mill, West Main Street, Honeoye Falls. This sturdy old stone mill has been converted into an attractive restaurant, overlooking the stream that furnished power for the early industries of the village. This appreciative adaptive use characterizes the attitude of the community in recognizing its historic and scenic resources.

10

CONCLUSION

It has been nearly two centuries since the building of permanent structures began in Monroe County. In the history of human settlement, this is a brief interval, but in upstate New York it represents development from primitive beginnings to modern achievements of vast size and technical sophistication. Not many generations separate the builders of the brick Phoenix Hotel in Pittsford from those of the brick campus of the Rochester Institute of Technology. Within a single lifetime, in fact, building technology advanced from the raising of timber barns to the erection of high steel office buildings.

112. **A Century of Rochester Building:** Powers Building (1869), Crossroads Building (1969), and Monroe County Courthouse (1894–96).

The cultural wealth of Monroe County, its patrimony from prior generations, is, perhaps, made most evident in daily life by familiar surroundings from the past. They reveal the tastes and skills of many decades and remain as a testament of confidence from those who built permanent structures for the future. It is for us to conserve and convey to the future this message from the past, and to contribute to the inheritance some evidence of our own time, its accomplishments and values. Buildings become more than facts of history; they are to be read as expressions of people who built them, varying from the simple folk art of rural cottages and mills to the urbane subtleties of cultivated taste.

In looking at history, each generation re-evaluates the past, selecting what it finds interesting, attractive, or useful. Certain periods and styles are considered to be more meritorious of preservation than are others, but because tastes will always change, the interests of preservation should be broader than the tastes of one's own time. Buildings that may appear distasteful to some of us may prove to be more valued by another generation. In looking at our surroundings, we should remember that every era built what represented to its builders a realization of their technical capabilities and an expression of their cultural values.

Important as many of these works are individually—and some are of national significance—a more general conclusion may be derived from this visit to Monroe County. The regional community here is closely related to its habitat, as is demonstrated by the Landmark Society of Western New York. This very successful model of community organization, from initial appreciation for a single historical building and dedication to its preservation and maintenance, has evolved over three decades a broader concern for the larger place, the neighborhood, the county. This book has attempted to convey such an awareness of the character of Monroe County as a place in which to live with a sense of identity derived from the past, seeing familiar surroundings in a newly appreciative way.

This limited survey has been intended not so much as an inventory, even partial, of all of the buildings of importance in the county, but as a visit to several neighborhoods, villages, and urban districts that have value as *places*—areas that retain individuality and give variety to an environment that otherwise might become monotonously mass-produced. The character of a place derives in part from its accumulation of history, in part from the accretion of its built environment, from the arrangement of exterior spaces, trees and gardens, and certainly from the continuing evidence of loving care. Such a place is the expression of its people. The desirability of a place to live may be subtly measured by the ways in which those who live there express their attitudes about themselves and the place in which they live. A lived-in place in time portrays a people's personality. Many generations have left a wealth of lived-in places that enrich the character of Monroe County. This character is worth preserving.

APPENDIX 1

Chronological Listing of Monroe County Landmarks Mentioned in Text

Page references are printed in italic type. Numbers in boldface type refer to plates.

c. 1792 Stone-Tolan House (land acquired) *45*, **23, 24** Federal

c. 1810 Fletcher Steele House *33*, **15** Federal

c. 1812 Elliot House *34, 36* Federal

c. 1812–24 Phoenix Hotel *31*, **14** Federal

1816 Oliver Culver Tavern *60, 63*, **30** Federal

1816 William H. Guetersloh House *36* Federal

c. 1816 8 Rochester Street, Scottsville *203* Federal

1819 The "Little House" *33* Federal

c. 1820–25 Albert Palmer House *184*, **91** Federal

1822 The Spring House *43*, **19** Federal–Greek Revival

c. 1822 Stone Warehouse *16*, **8** Stone and timber commercial construction

1824 Judge John Bowman House *187*, **92** Federal

1824 St. Luke's Episcopal Church *126, 128, 130, 132*, **67, 69** Federal–Gothic Revival

1825 Congregational church, Clarkson *181* Federal

1826 Sylvanus Lathrop House *33–34*, **16** Federal

1827 Wilcox House (original portion) *222*, **110** Federal

c. 1827 Upper Mill *225*, **111** Stone and timber commercial construction

1828 Simeon B. Jewett House *189*, **1, 93** Federal

c. 1829 Lower Mill *218*, **108** Stone and timber commercial construction

1830 Ira Buck House *34* Federal

1835 25 South Main Street, Pittsford *36* Federal

1835 Campbell-Whittlesey House *154, 156, 159–60*, **77–79** Greek Revival

1835 Exchange Hotel *210*, **104** Federal

1836 1836 House, Genesee Country Museum *214*, **106** Federal

1837 Jonathan Child House *141–43, 148*, **70** Greek Revival

c. 1837 Hervey Ely House *146, 148*, **72** Greek Revival

1838 Mount Hope Cemetery dedicated *175*

1838–41 Woodside (Silas O. Smith House) *79–80, 83*, **40** Greek Revival

1839 Colonel Henry Cady House *152* Greek Revival

1839 James Hawks House (remodeled as Ellwanger residence) *166*, **82**

1840 Elihu Kirby House *9*, **2** Greek Revival

1840 David Lee House *190*, **94** Greek Revival

c. 1840 John Dorr House *209*, **103** Greek Revival

c. 1840 William Pitkin House *83* Greek Revival

c. 1841 Lemuel Haskell House *189* Greek Revival

1841–42 St. John's Episcopal Church *225* Greek Revival–Gothic Revival

1842 District No. 6 Schoolhouse *36*, **17** Greek Revival

1842 Aaron Erickson House (Erickson-Perkins, Genesee Valley Club) *84*, **41** Greek Revival

1842 Presbyterian church, Honeoye Falls *221*, **109** Greek Revival

1843–46 St. Joseph's Roman Catholic Church *94, 97*, **48, 50** Greek Revival

c. 1844 Amon Bronson House *151–52*, **74** Greek Revival

1846 Edson House *203–4*, **100** Greek Revival

1848 William Churchill House *152*, **74** Greek-Italianate

1849–50 Fletcher Steele House (addition) *33*, **15** Federal–Greek Revival

1850 John Bowman House *193, 195*, **95** Greek Revival

c. 1850 10 Rochester Street, Scottsville *203*, **99** Greek Revival

c. 1850 Isaac Loomis House *151* Gothic Revival

c. 1850 Ward House *97–98*, **52** Italianate

1852 138 South Fitzhugh Street, Rochester *154*, **76** Greek Revival

1852–54 Charles F. Bissell House *76* Gothic Revival

1853 Dr. Hartwell Carver House *34* Gothic Revival

1853 Clarkson Academy *183*, **90** Greek Revival

1854 Ellwanger and Barry Nursery Office *169*, **3, 83** Gothic Revival

1854 Morgan-Manning House *196*, **97** Italianate

1854 Warner Castle *178*, **89**

1855–57 Patrick Barry House *171–72*, **83–86** Italianate

1856 Bates-Ryder House *60*, **29** Italianate

1860, 1863 The Depot *38*, **18**

1860 Small chapel, Mount Hope Cemetery *175*, **87** Gothic Revival

c. 1860 1 Main Street, Brockport *195*, **96**

1861 Anderson Hall, old campus *87*, **45** Second Empire

1861 Presbyterian church, Pittsford *36* Italianate

1864 Emmet Hollister House *163*, **80** Italianate

1864–73 Immaculate Conception Roman Catholic Church *152* Italianate

1865 Harris-Spencer House *72*, **36** Italianate

1865 Charles E. Hart House *163*, **80** Second Empire

1868 Christ Episcopal Church *34* Gothic Revival

1868 Former Sacred Heart Academy *87* Gothic-mixed

1868 Hiram Sibley House *84*, **42** Italianate (remodeled, Georgian eclectic)

1903 James S. Watson Library *87*, **44** Eclectic–18th-century French

1904, 1911, 1926 Sibley, Lindsay & Curr Company *93*, **47, 48** Modern

1905 George Eastman House *74*, **37** Eclectic-Georgian

1906 William E. Sloan House *69* Eclectic-Georgian

1907–8 Edward Boynton House *63–64*, *66*, **31, 32** Modern

1908 First Universalist Church *104*, *106*, *108*, **56, 57** Eclectic-Lombard

1910 Bevier Memorial Building *146* Eclectic

c. 1910 Gleason Works (entrance facade) *56*, **28** Eclectic-neoclassical

1913 35 East Boulevard, Rochester *66* Eclectic

1913 Memorial Art Gallery, old campus *91*, **46** Eclectic–Italian Renaissance

1913 Henry M. Stern House *56*, *60* Eclectic-Tudor

1916 Lincoln Avenue School *23*

1917 Garden loggia of George Eastman House *74* Eclectic

1920 Knollwood Drive, Pittsford *43*, **20** Eclectic

1920 Douglas Road, Rochester *69*, **33** Eclectic

1922 Herbert Stern House *69* Eclectic

1922 Eastman Theater *98*, **53** Eclectic

1924 First National Bank (formerly Monroe County Savings Bank) *116* Eclectic–Classic Revival

1925 Hiram Sibley Building *84*, **43** Eclectic–English baroque

1926 Cutler Union, old campus *91*, **46** Eclectic-Gothic

1928 Rochester Savings Bank *94*, **48, 49** Eclectic-Roman

1929 Times Square Building *23–24*, **11** Modernistic

1936 Rundel Memorial Library *113* Modernistic

1950 Dryden Theater *74* Eclectic-Georgian

1952–63 Temple Beth El *45* Modern

1958 St. Louis Roman Catholic Church *34* Modern

1962, 1970 First Unitarian Church *45*, *47*, **25** Modern

1962 Midtown Plaza *101*, **54** Modern

1965 Liberty Pole *93*, **47** Modern

1967 Temple Sinai *45*, **22** Modern

1968 Memorial Art Gallery (addition) *91*, **46** Modern

1968 Rochester Institute of Technology (completion) *198*, **98** Modern

1968 Strasenburgh Planetarium *79*, **39** Modern

1968 Xerox Building *103*, **55, 56** Modern

1969 Crossroads Building *116, 118*, **63** Modern

1970 Marine Midland Bank Building *103*, **55** Modern

1971 Robert H. Antell House *24*, **12** Modern

1973 Lincoln First Bank Building *103*, **13** Modern

APPENDIX 2

Works of Prominent Architects in Monroe County

Page references are printed in italic type. Numbers in boldface type refer to plates.

Josiah R. Brady
    1824 St. Luke's Episcopal Church *126, 128, 130, 132,* **67, 69**

S. P. Hastings
    1837 Jonathan Child House (?) *141–43, 148,* **70**
    c. 1837 Hervey Ely House (?) *146, 148,* **72**

Alfred M. Badger
    1838–41 Woodside (Silas O. Smith House) *79–80, 83,* **40**

Nehemiah Osborn
    c. 1840 William Pitkin House (?) *83*
    1842 Aaron Erickson House *84,* **41**

Martin Pierce
    1842 Presbyterian Church, Honeoye Falls (?) *221,* **109**

Jones and Nevins
    1843–46 St. Joseph's Roman Catholic Church *94, 97,* **48, 50**

Henry Searle
    1849 Brewster-Burke House (?) *143, 145, 148,* **71**

Andrew Jackson Warner
    1852–54 Charles F. Bissell House *76*
    1869 Powers Building *114, 116,* **58–62, 63**
    1871 First Presbyterian Church *146*
    1872–73 Rochester Free Academy *130, 132,* **67**

Gordon and Kaelber
    1922 Eastman Theater (with McKim, Mead and White) *98*, **53**
    1926 Cutler Union *91*, **46**

Mowbray and Uffinger
    1924 First National Bank (formerly Monroe County Savings Bank) *116*

Shepley, Bulfinch and Abbot (Boston)
    1925 Hiram Sibley Building *84*, **43**

Voorhees, Gmelin and Walker (New York)
    1929 Times Square Building (with Carl C. Ade) *23–24*, **11**

T. W. Moore
    1950 Dryden Theater *74*

Percival Goodman (New York)
    1952–63 Temple Beth El *45*

Victor Gruen Associates (Los Angeles)
    1962 Midtown Plaza *101*, **54**

Louis I. Kahn (Philadelphia)
    1962, 1970 First Unitarian Church *45, 47*, **25**

James H. Johnson
    1965 Liberty Pole *93*, **47**
    1967 Temple Sinai *45*, **22**
    1971 Robert H. Antell House *24*, **12**

Lawrence B. Anderson (Boston)

Edward Larrabee Barnes (New York)

Kevin Roche and John Dinkeloo (Connecticut)

Hugh Stubbins (Cambridge, Mass.)

Harry M. Weese (Chicago)

APPENDIX 3

Official Designations of Historic Buildings

The following list of historic buildings is not complete; the compilation of such a list is ongoing. Buildings are not listed in order of priority.

Asterisks designate properties owned by the Landmark Society. Daggers indicate properties transferred by the Landmark Society (or by its subsidiary, the Genesee Landmarks Foundation) with restrictive covenants.

Page references are printed in italic type. Numbers in boldface type refer to plates.

National Historic Landmarks

Susan B. Anthony House, 17 Madison Street (off 560 West Main Street), Rochester. Susan B. Anthony lived here for forty years, during which time she worked for the enfranchisement of women. The house is open to the public Wednesday through Saturday, from 11:00 a.m. to 4:00 p.m. (not included in book)

George Eastman House *74*, **37**

National Register of Historic Places

Historic District: Jonathan Child House† and Brewster-Burke House* Historic District *141–43, 148,* **70**; *143, 145, 148,* **71**

Bevier Memorial Building *146*

Campbell-Whittlesey House* *154, 156, 159–60,* **77–79**

Daisy Flour Mill Historic District, 1880 Blossom Road, Penfield

Hervey Ely House *146, 148,* **72**

Federal Building *122, 125,* **64, 65**

First Presbyterian Church *146*

City of Rochester Designations

GLOSSARY OF ARCHITECTURAL TERMS

Numbers in parentheses refer to plates.

Arcade: A series of arches linked end to end (65).

Balustrade: A railing of classical character, most typically composed of urn-shaped vertical members (44).

Beaded mortar joints: Interstices of masonry, usually brick, tooled so as to result in a decorative, concave profile between parallel incisions.

Board and batten: Vertical wood siding with small wood strips covering the joints.

Capital: In classical architecture, the decorative head of a column (70).

Ceiling molding: An ornamental, raised band, usually of plaster. Characteristic of the Greek Revival and subsequent styles, work of this sort became particularly elaborate towards the mid-century (85).

Chancel: The less public part of a church of traditional form, usually separated by a rail or screen, including the choir and altar. Most typically in a cruciform plan, this would be the head of the cross, extending eastward beyond the nave and transepts (101).

Clapboard: Horizontal wood siding, saw-tooth in profile due to overlapping or tapering of boards (103).

Coffered: Generally referring to a ceiling, decorated with a regular pattern of rectangular indentations (53).

Colonnette: A miniature column (1).

Column: A vertical support, circular in plan. In classical architecture it is composed of a shaft, a decorative capital, and, sometimes, a base (70).

Console: A bracket of scroll-like profile (77).

Corbeled: Projected out in steps by advancing one course of masonry slightly forward of that below it (110).

Corinthian: The most elaborate of three major classical orders of architecture, identified most prominently by representation of foliage on column capitals (70).

Cornice: A projection, usually composed of moldings, at the top of a wall (10).

Course: A horizontal row of blocks, bricks, cobbles, or other material (17).

Crenellations, crenellated: A toothed notching of the top of a wall, originally for defense of battlements, hence characteristic of castles (89).

Cresting: Decorative metal work, generally appearing as a railing surmounting a roof. This was a feature most associated with the Second Empire style (5).

Crockets, crocketed: In Gothic architecture, projecting hook or leaflike forms found on inclined corners of spires or gables (67).

Cupola: A decorative superstructure surmounting a roof, usually hipped. Typical of the Greek Revival and Italianate styles, the glazed roof pavilion sometimes provided ventilation and frequently was used as a scenic outlook (75).

Doric: The simplest of three major classical orders (72).

Dormer: Projections from a sloping roof incorporating a vertical window (37).

Eaves: Roof projections, overhanging the wall to carry water away from it. In Federal and Greek Revival work, "boxed eaves" are usually employed (93), with a horizontal bottom ("soffit") blocked down from the inclined rafters. Sometimes, particularly in later work, the slope of the rafters is left visible (73).

Eaves brackets: Decorative, frequently nonstructural supports. One of the most familiar marks of the Italianate style (4).

Entablature: In classical architecture, that elaboration of the lintel and eaves carried by columns (70).

Entasis: A Greek term referring to the subtle curvature of the sides of a column that gives it an irregular tapering so that it is not a simple cylinder (92).

Escutcheon: A decorative plate covering the juncture of a projection, such as a door handle or a ceiling chandelier, from a larger surface. Most typically it is a rosette-like sleeve. Together with elaborate ceiling moldings, this became a feature of mid-nineteenth-century ceilings (86).

Facade: The face of a building, as it is seen horizontally (2).

Fanlight: A form of transom that is arched. In Federal work the curvature generally is elliptical (1).

Flat arch: Seemingly a contradiction in terms, this refers to a lintel that, instead of being a single piece, is made up of a number of pieces, formed segmentally to provide an arching action (94).

Fluting: Decorative parallel grooves, most commonly associated with columns or pilasters (70).

Frieze band: In Greek Revival architecture, a broad band in the entablature into which decorative iron grills often were inserted (100).

Gable: The upper portion of the end wall of a building with pitched roofs, made triangular by the inclined planes of the roof (73).

Hipped roof: A flattened pyramid in form, with roof planes sloping in four directions, in contrast to the simpler gable roof with only two roof planes (75).

Ionic: One of three major classical orders, identified most commonly by scroll-like column capitals (1, 77).

Lintel: The block of stone or other material placed over a wall opening to carry the wall above (16).

Mansard roof: Of French origin, identified in this country with the Second Empire, it is a form of hipped roof, made compound by addition of a lower slope that is nearly vertical. This forms a transition between the wall and a flatter hipped roof covering the upper portion and provides more attic space (45).

Mosaics: Pictoral designs made up of fragments of colored glass or ceramics (49).

Mullion: A vertical division between two or more windows (20).

Mutins: Divider strips separating panes of glass in a window (23).

Ogee arch: In late Gothic work, an arch of double curvature, the lower part of each side being concave; the upper, convex (67).

Orders: In classical architecture, a set of related components consisting of the column and its own parts, together with portions of the building serving as its base and the entablature, or that part of the building carried by the columns. The Doric,

Ionic, and Corinthian are the most familiar classical orders, each varying in these components, and there are other minor orders as well.

Pediment: In classical architecture, the flattened triangle appearing in the gable above a horizontal entablature (70).

Pilaster: A simulation of a column projecting from a wall. If the projection is rounded, it is termed an "engaged column" (43); if it is rectangular in plan, with a flat rather than curved surface, it is termed a "pilaster" (44).

Pillar: A vertical support, usually of stone. To distinguish it from a "column," which is circular in plan, the term "pillar" is generally limited to piers that are square or rectangular in plan (46).

Pinnacles: In Gothic and Romanesque architecture, vertical projections above a wall or tower, usually used in groups, resembling miniature spired towers (67).

Portico: A porch of classical character, with columns and entablature, sometimes with pediment (2, 70).

Quoins: Blocks, originally of stone, laid up at the corner of a building. Emphasized by projection from the face of the wall, sometimes with their corners chamfered off, or by being of a different material from the rest of the wall. They characteristically provide a decorative, toothed pattern (17). Sometimes they were imitated in wood (23).

Regency: A stylistic reference to the period of English architecture roughly equivalent to the Federal in the United States. It followed the Georgian and preceded the Victorian, and is characterized by small-scaled elegance.

Romanesque: A general reference to the round-arched architecture of the era between the fifth and mid-twelfth centuries. This was an influence on the American architect H. H. Richardson, and the style prevalent in the 1880s.

Side lights: Small, vertical windows on each side of the doorway (1).

Stepped gables: Projection of an end wall, usually of masonry, above the slope of the roof (14). Sometimes termed "crow stepped," frequently incorporating chimneys, they are a characteristic feature of Federal architecture in upstate New York, associated particularly with the Dutch influence of the Hudson and Mohawk valleys, although such gables also may be found in Scotland.

Transept: In a cross-shaped church, the arms of the cross (101).

Transom: A panel, usually glazed and sometimes operating for ventilation, over a door, separated from it by a transom bar. Generally refers to a rectangular element (94). The familiar curved form is known as a fanlight.

Turret: A small tower, generally cylindrical, attached to or rising from a larger building (26).

Verge boards: Sometimes called "barge boards," the term refers generally to Gothic Revival decorative trim of the gable, where a board applied to the edge of the projecting roof of a gable would be cut into a lacy pattern (21).

Wainscot, wainscoting: A wooden paneling, usually covering the lower portion of an interior wall, or, by extension, a similar covering of another material (101).

BIBLIOGRAPHY

Many works of architectural history consider the periods and styles mentioned in this book. Listed below are a few introductory books for the general reader.

Architecture Worth Saving in New York State series:

Dutchess County Planning Board. *Landmarks of Dutchess County, 1683–1867.* New York: New York State Council on the Arts, 1969.

Foerster, Bernd M. *Architecture Worth Saving in Rensselaer County, New York.* Troy, N.Y.: Rensselaer Polytechnic Institute, 1965.

Kelly, Virginia B., O'Connell, Merrilyn R., Olney, Stephen S., and Reig, Johanna R. *Wood and Stone, Landmarks of the Upper Mohawk Region.* Utica, N.Y.: Central New York Community Arts Council, 1972.

McKee, Harley J., with Earle, Patricia Day, Malo, Paul, and Andrews, Peter. *Architecture Worth Saving in Onondaga County.* Syracuse, N.Y.: Syracuse University School of Architecture, 1964.

Prokopoff, Stephen S., and Siegfried, Joan C. *The Nineteenth-century Architecture of Saratoga Springs.* New York: New York State Council on the Arts, 1970.

Related publications:

Everest, Allan S. *Our North Country Heritage, Architecture Worth Saving in Clinton and Essex Counties.* Plattsburgh, N.Y.: Tundra Books, 1972.

Montillon, Eugene D. *Historic Architecture in Broome County, New York and Vicinity.* Binghamton, N.Y.: Broome County Planning Department, Broome County Historical Society, 1972.

Wolfe, Andrew D., Hart, Isabella H., and Malo, Paul. *Architecture Worth Saving in Pittsford, Elegant Village.* Pittsford, N.Y.: Historic Pittsford, 1969.

Other publications with references to Monroe County buildings:

The Story of 40 Franklin Street, Main Office of Rochester Savings Bank. Scheible Press, 1967.

Comstock, Helen. *One Hundred Most Beautiful Rooms in America.* New York: Viking Press, 1958.

Costa, Erville. "Claude F. Bragdon, Architect, Stage Designer and Mystic." *Rochester History,* October, 1967.

France, Jean R., Merritt, Howard S., McKelvey, Blake, and Kennedy, Roger G. *A Rediscovery—Harvey Ellis: Artist, Architect.* Rochester, N.Y.: Memorial Art Gallery of the University of Rochester, 1972.

Hersey, Carl K. "The Architectural Origins of Woodside (1838)." Rochester, N.Y.: Rochester Historical Society, 1964.

Hitchcock, Henry-R. *In the Nature of Materials: The Buildings of Frank Lloyd Wright, 1887–1941.* New York: DeCapo Press, 1973.

Kimbrough, Lee S. "The Importance of the Wilder Building, the German Insurance Building, and the Ellwanger and Barry Building in the Development of Skeletal Construction in the United States." Unpublished manuscript. Rochester, N.Y.: University of Rochester, 1964.

Lipscomb, Mary Elizabeth. "The Architecture of Harvey Ellis in Rochester, New York." Master's thesis, University of Rochester, 1969.

McKelvey, Blake. *Rochester: The Water-Power City, 1812–1854.* Cambridge, Mass.: Harvard University Press, 1945.

————. *Rochester: The Flower City, 1855–1890.* Cambridge, Mass.: Harvard University Press, 1949.

————. *Rochester: The Quest for Quality, 1890–1925.* Cambridge, Mass.: Harvard University Press, 1956.

————. *Rochester: An Emerging Metropolis, 1925–1961.* Rochester, N.Y.: Christopher Press, 1961.

————. *Rochester on the Genesee: The Growth of a City.* Syracuse, N.Y.: Syracuse University Press, 1973.

————. "East Avenue's Turbulent History." *Rochester History,* April–July, 1966.

Schmidt, Carl F. *Architectural Mouldings*. Scottsville, N.Y., 1967.

———. *Cobblestone Architecture*. 1944.

———. *Cobblestone Masonry*. Scottsville, N.Y., 1966.

———. *Colonial and Post-Colonial Details*. Scottsville, N.Y., 1969.

———. *Fences, Gates and Garden Houses*. Rochester, N.Y., 1963.

———. *Greek Revival Architecture in the Rochester Area*. Scottsville, N.Y., 1946.

———. *Greek Revival Details*. Scottsville, N.Y., 1968.

———. *History of the Town of Wheatland*. Rochester, N.Y., 1953.

———. *The Octagon Fad*. Scottsville, N.Y., 1958.

———. *The Victorian Era in the United States*. Scottsville, N.Y., 1971.

Schmidt, Carl F. and Ann. *Architecture and Architects of Rochester, N.Y.* Rochester, N.Y.: Rochester Society of Architects, 1959.

———. *Jonathan Child and His House*. Rochester, N.Y., 1962.

Wolfe, Andrew D. *Views of Old Rochester and the Genessee Country, from Indian Days to 1918*. Pittsford, N.Y.: Phoenix Press, 1970.

General introductions to the architecture of the nineteenth and twentieth centuries in North America:

Gowans, Alan. *Images of American Living*. Philadelphia: Lippincott, 1964.

Hamlin, Talbot F. *Greek Revival Architecture in America*. New York: Oxford University Press, 1944.

Hitchcock, Henry-R. *Architecture, Nineteenth and Twentieth Centuries*. Baltimore, Md.: Penguin Books, 1958.

Morrison, Hugh. *Early American Architecture*. New York: Oxford University Press, 1952.

Whiffen, Marcus. *American Architecture*. Cambridge, Mass.: M.I.T. Press, 1969.

Published by the Landmark Society of Western New York:

Campbell-Whittlesey House. Rochester, N.Y.: Landmark Society of Western New York, 1971.

This is Rochester . . . The Third Ward Today. Rochester, N.Y.: Society for the Preservation of Landmarks in Western New York, 1965.

McKee, Harley J. *Amateur's Guide to Terms Commonly Used to Describe Historic Buildings.* Rochester, N.Y.: Landmark Society of Western New York, 1970.

Selden, Marjorie Ward. *The Interior Paint of the Campbell-Whittlesey House.* Rochester, N.Y.: Landmark Society of Western New York, 1970.

MAPS

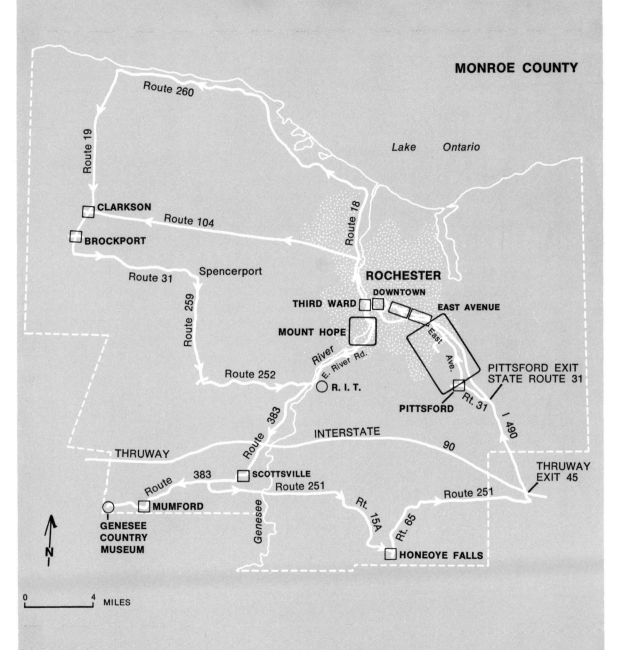

THE VILLAGE OF PITTSFORD

Page references are printed in italic type. Numbers in boldface italic type refer to plates.

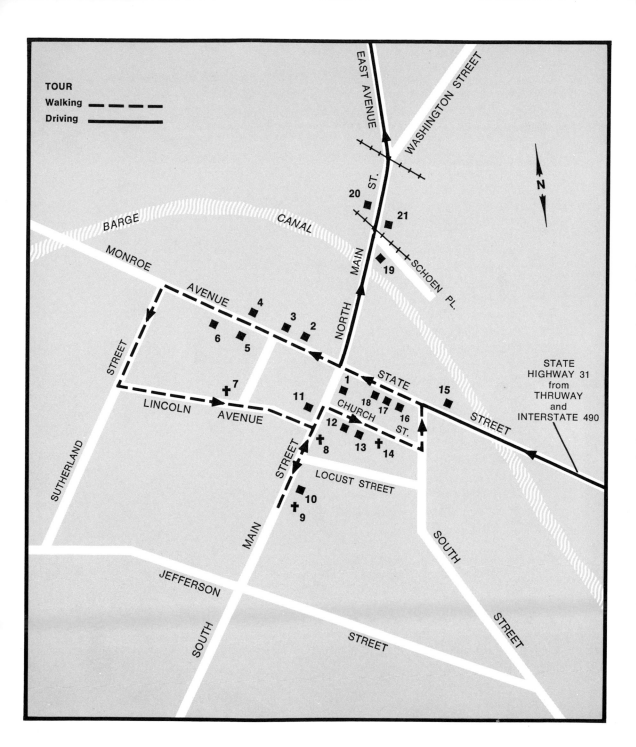

PITTSFORD TO DOWNTOWN ROCHESTER:

East Avenue and Its Environs

Page references are printed in italic type. Numbers in boldface italic type refer to plates.

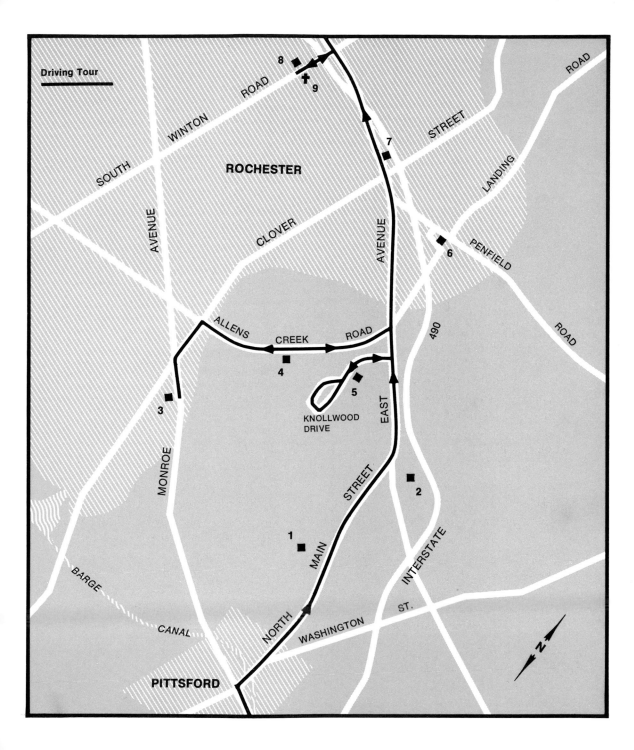

Driving Tour

ROCHESTER

ROAD

WINTON

SOUTH

AVENUE

CLOVER

AVENUE

STREET

ROAD

LANDING

PENFIELD

ROAD

8

9

7

6

ALLENS

CREEK

ROAD

4

KNOLLWOOD
DRIVE

5

EAST

490

3

MONROE

STREET

MAIN

2

1

INTERSTATE

BARGE

CANAL

NORTH

WASHINGTON

ST.

N

PITTSFORD

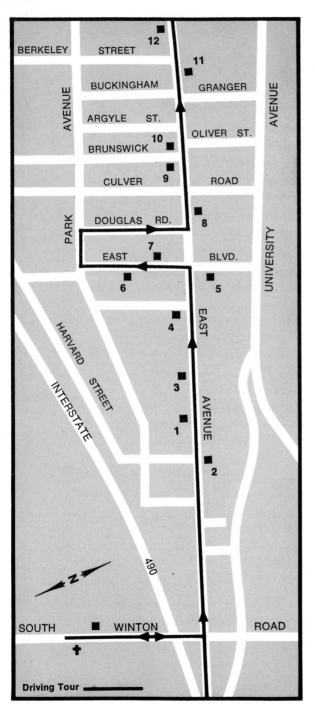

PITTSFORD TO DOWNTOWN ROCHESTER:

Unnumbered buildings are identified on the preceding map.
Page references are printed in italic type.
Numbers in boldface italic type refer to plates.

1 W. W. Chapin House,
1545 East Avenue, *54, 56,* **26**

2 Apartment building and beech tree,
1600 East Avenue, *56,* **27**

3 Henry M. Stern House,
1501 East Avenue, *56, 60*

4 Bates-Ryder House, 1399 East Avenue, *60,* **29**

5 Oliver Culver Tavern,
70 East Boulevard, *60, 63,* **30**

6 Edward Boynton House,
16 East Boulevard, *63–64, 66,* **31, 32**

7 35 East Boulevard, *66*

8 William E. Sloan House, 1250 East Avenue, *69*

9 Herbert Stern House, 2 Brunswick Street, *69*

10 Jesse W. Lindsay House, 1163 East Avenue, *69*

11 Wilson Soule House,
1050 East Avenue, *69–70, 72,* **34, 35**

12 Harris-Spencer House,
1005 East Avenue, *72,* **36**

East Avenue and Its Environs

1   George Eastman House,
      900 East Avenue, *74*, **37**
2   St. Paul's Episcopal Church,
      841 East Avenue, *74*
3   Leon Stern House, 740 East Avenue, *74*
4   727 East Avenue, *74, 76,* **38**
5   Colonel Henry A. Strong House,
      693 East Avenue, *76*
6   Charles F. Bissell House, 666 East Avenue, *76*
7   Strasenburgh Planetarium,
      663 East Avenue, *79*, **39**
8   Albert Vogt House, 56 East Avenue, *79*
9   Third Presbyterian Church,
      East Avenue and Meigs Street, *79*
10   Woodside, the Silas O. Smith House,
      485 East Avenue, *79–80, 83,* **40**
11   William Pitkin House, 474 East Avenue, *83*
12   Aaron Erickson House,
      421 East Avenue, *84,* **41**
13   Hiram Sibley House, 400 East Avenue, *84,* **42**
14   Hiram Sibley Building,
      311 Alexander Street, *84,* **43**
15   Fitch Building, 315 Alexander Street, *84*
16   Gleason Works,
      1000 University Avenue, *56, 84,* **28**
17   Former Sacred Heart Academy,
      8 Prince Street, *87*
18   William Cogswell House, 7 Prince Street, *87*
19   James S. Watson Library,
      9 Prince Street, *87,* **44**
20   Anderson Hall, 75 College Avenue, *87,* **45**
21   Cutler Union, 560 University Avenue, *91,* **46**
22   Memorial Art Gallery,
      490 University Avenue, *91,* **46**

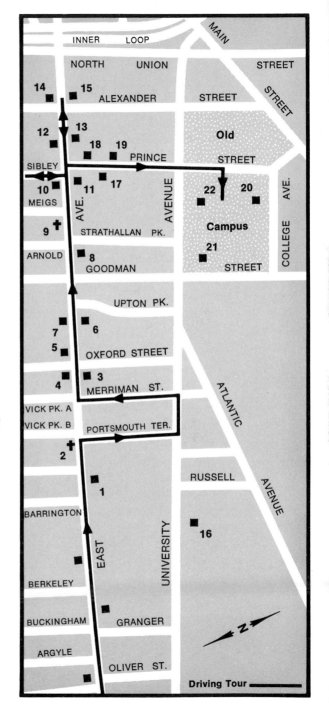

DOWNTOWN ROCHESTER:

From the Liberty Pole to Washington Square

Unnumbered buildings are identified on the preceding map.

Page references are printed in italic type. Numbers in boldface italic type refer to plates.

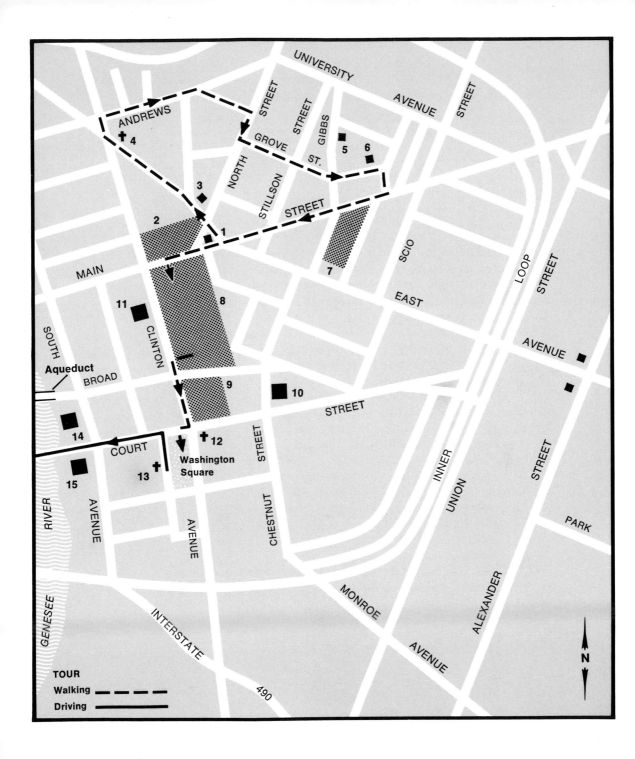

UNIVERSITY

STREET

STREET

AVENUE

STREET

ANDREWS

✝ 4

GROVE

STREET

STILLSON ST.

NORTH

GIBBS

■ 5

■ 6

STREET

3 ◆

STREET

1 ◆

7

SCIO

MAIN

2

EAST

LOOP

STREET

SOUTH

11 ■

CLINTON

8

AVENUE

■

Aqueduct

BROAD

9

10 ■

STREET

■

14 ■

COURT

STREET

13 ✝

12 ✝
Washington
Square

INNER

15 ■

RIVER

AVENUE

AVENUE

CHESTNUT STREET

UNION

STREET

PARK

GENESEE

INTERSTATE

MONROE

ALEXANDER

490

AVENUE

N

TOUR
Walking ▬ ▬ ▬
Driving ▬▬▬▬

Unnumbered buildings are identified on the preceding map.

Page references are printed in italic type. Numbers in boldface italic type refer to plates.

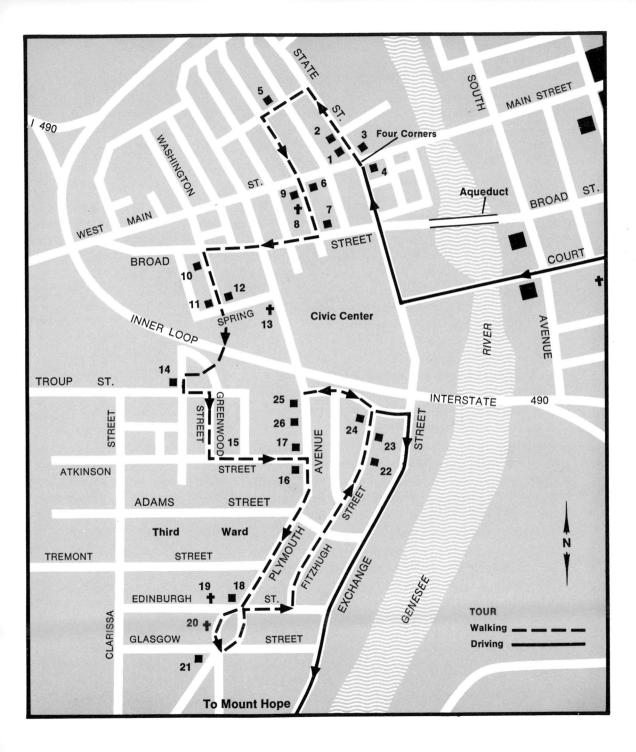

MOUNT HOPE

Page references are printed in italic type. Numbers in boldface italic type refer to plates.

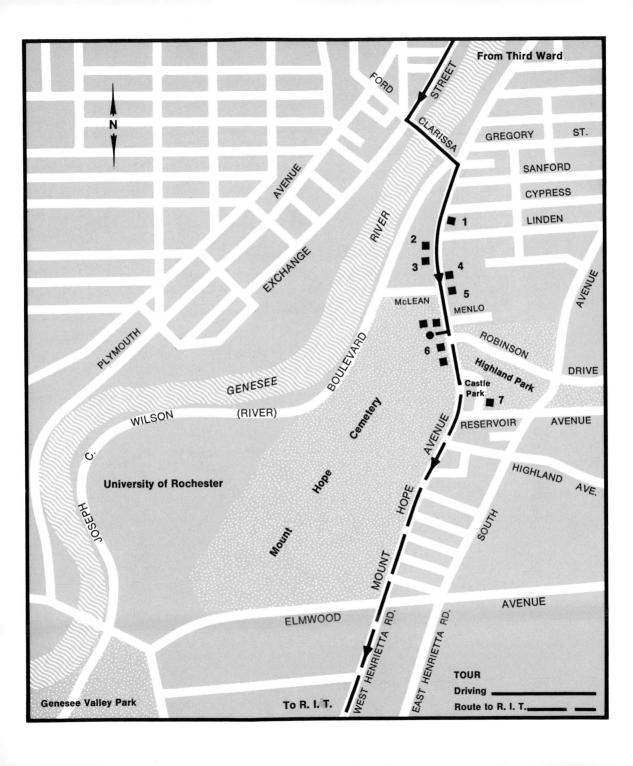

N

From Third Ward

FORD

STREET

CLARISSA

GREGORY   ST.

SANFORD

CYPRESS

LINDEN

■ 1

RIVER

2 ■

3 ■   ■ 4

■ 5

AVENUE

EXCHANGE

McLEAN   MENLO

AVENUE

■■●   ROBINSON

6 ■

■   DRIVE

Highland Park

BOULEVARD

Castle
Park   ■ 7

PLYMOUTH

GENESEE

(RIVER)

WILSON

RESERVOIR   AVENUE

HIGHLAND   AVE.

University of Rochester

Cemetery

Hope

Mount

MOUNT   HOPE   AVENUE

SOUTH

JOSEPH
C.

AVENUE

ELMWOOD

To R. I. T.

WEST HENRIETTA RD.

EAST HENRIETTA RD.

TOUR

Driving ―――――

Route to R. I. T. ――― ―

Genesee Valley Park

CLARKSON

Page references are printed in italic type.

Numbers in boldface italic type refer to plates.

1 Congregational church, 8339 Ridge Road West, *181*
2 Clarkson Academy, 8343 Ridge Road West, *183*, ***90***
3 Lewis Swift House, 8265 Ridge Road West, *184*
4 Albert Palmer House, 8251 Ridge Road West, *184*, ***91***
5 Cobblestone shop, 3726 Lake Road, *187*
6 Judge John Bowman House, 3797 Lake Road, *187*, ***92***
7 Simeon B. Jewett House, 3779 Lake Road, *189*, ***1, 93***
8 Henry Martyn House, 3773 Lake Road, *189*
9 Lemuel Haskell House, 3759 Lake Road, *189*
10 David Lee House, 3749 Lake Road, *190*, ***94***
11 John Bowman House, 3741 Lake Road, *193*, *195*, ***95***

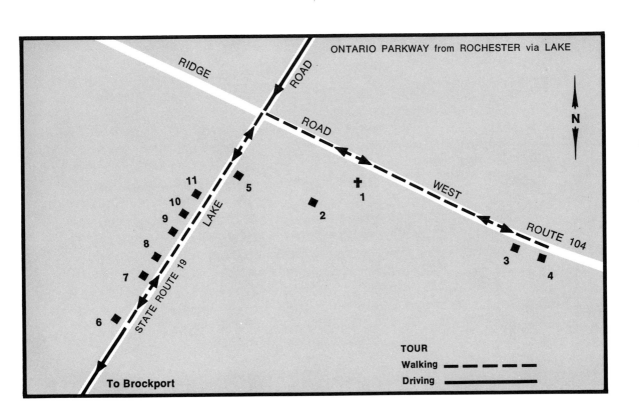

RIDGE

ONTARIO PARKWAY from ROCHESTER via LAKE

ROAD

ROAD

WEST

N

5

11

10

9

8

7

6

LAKE

STATE ROUTE 19

1

2

3

4

ROUTE 104

TOUR

Walking

Driving

To Brockport

271

BROCKPORT

Page references are printed in italic type. Numbers in boldface italic type refer to plates.

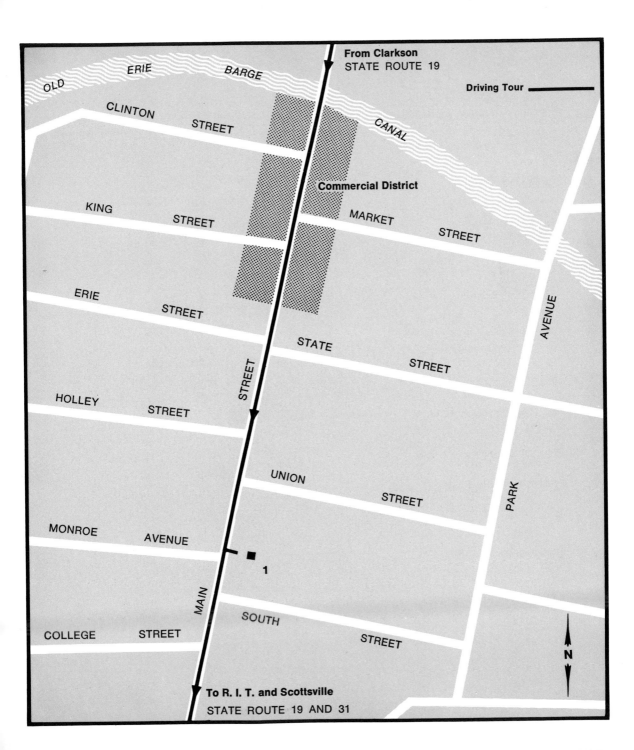

SCOTTSVILLE

Page references are printed in italic type.

Numbers in boldface italic type refer to plates.

1   Old inn (now an automatic laundry), 17 Main Street, *200*
2   Cobblestone and brick commercial buildings (now
    Regional Valley Agency), 16 Main Street, *200*
3   8 Rochester Street, *203*
4   10 Rochester Street, *203*, ***99***
5   Edson House, 7 Rochester Street, *203–4*, ***100***
6   Grace Episcopal Church, Browns Avenue, *204, 206, 209*, ***7, 101***
7   Schoolhouse, Browns Avenue, *209*
8   Union Presbyterian Church, Browns Avenue, *209*, ***102***
9   John Dorr House, 17 Church Street, *209*, ***103***

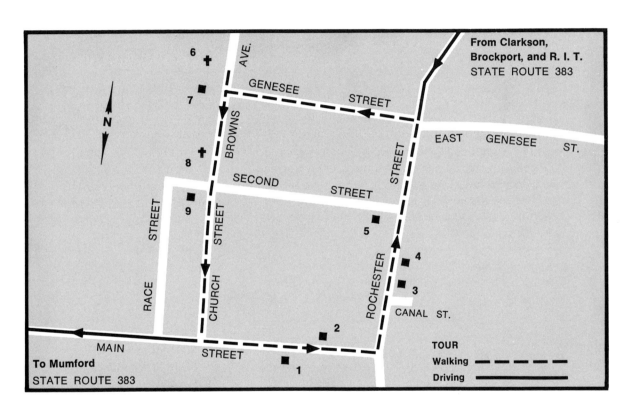

From Clarkson,
Brockport, and R. I. T.
STATE ROUTE 383

6 ✝

AVE.

GENESEE

STREET

7 ■

BROWNS

8 ✝

SECOND

STREET

STREET

EAST   GENESEE   ST.

9 ■

RACE

STREET

CHURCH

STREET

5 ■

ROCHESTER

4 ■

3 ■

CANAL ST.

2 ■

TOUR

Walking

Driving

MAIN

STREET

1 ■

To Mumford
STATE ROUTE 383

N

HONEOYE FALLS

Page references are printed in italic type.

Numbers in boldface italic type refer to plates.

1   13 Maplewood Avenue, *225*
2   Lower Mill, 61 North Main Street, *218*, ***108***
3   Presbyterian church, 27 North Main Street, *221*, ***109***
4   Wilcox House, 3 North Main Street, *222*, ***110***
5   Upper Mill, West Main Street, *225*, ***111***
6   St. John's Episcopal Church, Episcopal Avenue, *225*
7   37 Ontario Street, *225*, ***6***

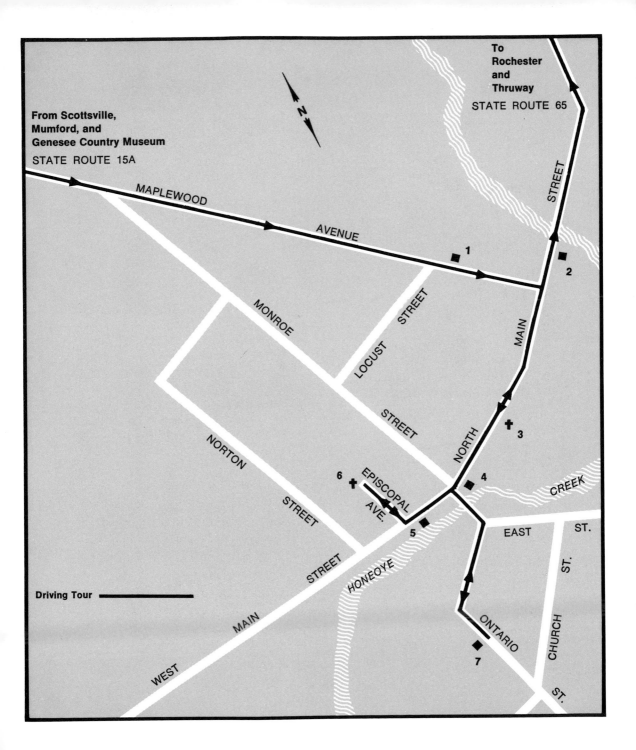

From Scottsville,
Mumford, and
Genesee Country Museum
STATE ROUTE 15A

To
Rochester
and
Thruway
STATE ROUTE 65

MAPLEWOOD

AVENUE

MONROE

LOCUST

STREET

STREET

MAIN

STREET

NORTH

STREET

NORTON

STREET

STREET

WEST

MAIN

HONEOYE

EPISCOPAL

AVE.

EAST

CREEK

ST.

CHURCH

ST.

ST.

ONTARIO

1

2

3

4

5

6

7

N

Driving Tour

LANDMARKS OF ROCHESTER AND MONROE COUNTY

A Guide to Neighborhoods and Villages

has been set in twelve-point Linotype Bodoni Book leaded
one point by Dix Typesetting Company; printed by offset
on 80-pound Warren's Lustro Offset Enamel Dull by the
Rapoport Printing Corporation, using the Stonetone process for the photographs; bound by the Vail-Ballou Press
using Columbia Bayside Vellum stamped in aluminum foil
for the hardbound edition and 100-pound Warren's Lustro
Offset Enamel Dull Cover for the softcover edition; and
published by

SYRACUSE UNIVERSITY PRESS